"*The Horizon of Faith* is a book which explores both the richness for discipleship and the cosmic vision of John's gospel. It stems as all good books should do from the intrigue of the author, who is both a distinguished theologian and someone experienced in pastoral and preaching ministry in a local church. Go on this journey and find new horizons opening up for faith and understanding God and the world."
—DAVID WILKINSON,
Professor of Theology and Religion, Durham University

"*The Horizon of Faith* is a refreshing take on John's gospel. Fresh, insightful and accessible, this book is the perfect companion for those who love the gospels. If you want to go deeper, this book will take you there."
—MIKE ROYAL, BISHOP,
Pentecostal Church, United Kingdom

"This book is a wonderful impulse for one's own further thinking, for general and deep questions about Christian life, also in contemporary times—and in a way that is not as unfortunately pressing or tendential as many other publications. There could be a need and a gap in the German market exactly for personal, academically based, and exegetically answerable literature that is not overloaded with methodology, didactics, and specialists' details—especially commenting on St. John's Gospel! Interested and—in the best sense—pious readers could find here exactly the insight and impulses they are looking for."
—ANDREAS OHLEMACHER,
Church Executive for Ecumenical and Theological Studies, German National Council of the Lutheran World Federation

"This is a distinctive work in which we encounter a unique perspective on St. John's Gospel that transcends the format of a traditional commentary. The author, who is both a scientist and priest, offers a deeply personal meditation that bridges the spiritual and scientific realms, a perspective especially relevant in our modern era. This volume will be accessible and at times gently challenging for a diverse readership—from those simply wishing a basic insight into the distinctive themes of the gospel to preachers seeking fresh starting points for homiletic preparation. The author's scientific background brings an added dimension to the work, opening up ideas related to the cosmic dimension of the Christ of John's Gospel. The timing of this publication holds special significance in this year when we mark the 1700th anniversary of the Council of Nicaea as Dr. Krauss considers at many points how this New Testament writing was key to shaping the Church's later doctrines of the Incarnation and the Trinity."

—DAVID HAMID,
Retired Suffragan Bishop, Anglican Diocese in Europe

"A stimulating introduction to the richness of theology in John. The Gospel according to John is a fascinating piece of literature, so theologically rich and challenging that new perspectives and insights will continue to enrich our reading and understanding of 'the light that shines in the darkness, and the darkness has not overcome it' (John 1:5). In *The Horizon of Faith: Rediscovering the Gospel of John*, Andrew Krauss has given us a short but very stimulating introduction to the world of John's theological universe. He has a fresh and stimulating capacity to sort out and follow some important threads as they develop through the gospel and also to open up to a wider understanding of the background in the Old Testament world, as well as appreciating the seeds for the later process of doctrinal development, especially given John's 'high' Christology and view of the Trinity. This is very important as the church celebrates the 1700th anniversary of the Council of

Nicaea in 325. There is also a basic pastoral tone in his presentation, opening up possibilities both for stimulating conversations and for preaching. Helping us in seeking the truth, he concludes with some noteworthy reflections on the tension and ambiguity in John's Gospel, focusing on the tension between a limited and an universal understanding of salvation, and reflecting on these tensions as part of our maturing as followers of Christ."

—TOR BERGER JØRGENSEN,
Former Bishop, Diocese of Sør-Hålogaland, Church of Norway

The Horizon of Faith

The Horizon of Faith

Encountering the Gospel of John

ANDREW KRAUSS

RESOURCE *Publications* • Eugene, Oregon

THE HORIZON OF FAITH
Encountering the Gospel of John

Copyright © 2025 Andrew Krauss. All rights reserved. Except for brief quotations in critical publications or reviews, no part of this book may be reproduced in any manner without prior written permission from the publisher. Write: Permissions, Wipf and Stock Publishers, 199 W. 8th Ave., Suite 3, Eugene, OR 97401.

Resource Publications
An Imprint of Wipf and Stock Publishers
199 W. 8th Ave., Suite 3
Eugene, OR 97401

www.wipfandstock.com

PAPERBACK ISBN: 979-8-3852-6464-3
HARDCOVER ISBN: 979-8-3852-6465-0
EBOOK ISBN: 979-8-3852-6466-7
VERSION NUMBER 12/18/25

Scripture quotations are from New Revised Standard Version Bible: Anglicized Edition, copyright © 1989, 1995 National Council of the Churches of Christ in the United States of America. Used by permission. All rights reserved worldwide.

To Anna, with deep gratitude for your love and support.

Contents

Acknowledgments | ix

Introduction | xi

Chapter 1 Holistic Overview: An End in the Beginning and a Beginning in the End | 1

Chapter 2 An Orientation Towards God's Dwelling Among Us: Calling, Inviting and Apportioning | 19

Chapter 3 John's High Christology: Trinitarian Witness and Indwelling Participation | 43

Chapter 4 Seeing the Wood for the Trees: Not Being Distracted From the Journey | 68

Chapter 5 Something Yet Greater: Openness to the Unfolding Beyondness | 91

Epilogue: Tension and Ambiguity in John | 117

Bibliography | 121

Acknowledgments

I would like to express my gratitude to all those who first encouraged me to commit this to writing, and to Helen Cameron, David Hamid, Tor Berger Jørgensen, Andreas Ohlemacher, Mike Royal, and David Wilkinson for reading and endorsing the final draft of the text itself.

Introduction

This book is principally the reflection of my deep interest in, and appreciation of, the Gospel of John, which has developed consistently over the last fifteen years or so. It is a gospel to which I have found myself constantly returning, both in my work as an ordained minister and as someone with a deep interest in theology. It is a gospel that seems to me to be of great relevance to many important life questions, and often with a certain subtlety that requires noting key connections and sometimes reading between the lines. So often have I expressed my particular intrigue about this gospel in both sermons and small group discussions that it has increasingly been suggested to me, by those alongside whom I have walked in the journey of faith, that I commit this intrigue to writing.

If I were to mention just one landmark event that drew my intrigue to this gospel in particular, it would be a "gospelathon," organized mainly as an informative social get-together in the parish in which I did my curacy. The idea of such an occasion is to hear, throughout the course of the best part of an entire day, with breaks at various points for a brief sharing of thoughts over refreshments, an entire book of the Bible read from beginning to end. This gives a view of the text as a whole that is obviously lacking when we simply hear an isolated extract read out at a service. It so happened that the organizers of the event had chosen the Gospel of John—hereafter referred to simply as John—and I am very glad they did, because having the whole gospel progressively read to me by the various participants over the course of several hours, and also seeing how others were struck by things they hadn't noticed about it before, was both a moving and an eye-opening experience.

It should be emphasized from the outset, however, that this is *not* intended as a "commentary," and for two main reasons: firstly, because my particular area is the theology-science interface and not biblical scholarship *per se*; secondly, because this is first and foremost an expression of intrigue that aims to reflect upon how the great depth of this gospel can accompany us all on our various journeys. I have deliberately avoided citing specifics from formal biblical commentaries, not least because everything in this book is, unless otherwise stated, a product of my own study of, and interest in, this text over the course of my journey so far. It *may* well be that many of the ideas and points raised can be found in the various formal commentaries available, but the presentation here remains the result of a personal journey of interest that I hope will be of use to others on their own journeys.

I am most grateful to all those who have encouraged me to present this in writing, and also to those whose writings I have cited in support of my own reflections. These writers are mainly ones who have had a very deep impact on my journey in the faith. I have cited them wherever I considered their particular input to resonate with the various thematic aspects of John reflected on here. Others I have cited simply because it is of more general interest to do so, and because I considered it helpful for the setting of the scene in various chapters.

In general, this gospel is of huge doctrinal import. If it were never to have been written, then the canonical material available for establishing a doctrine of the Trinity and the Incarnation would be severely impoverished. Readings from John also crop up on most of the big celebrations of the liturgical year. It has, certainly to my mind, a significant internal consistency and very far-reaching scope. What I aim to do in the five chapters that follow is to reflect on five particular "threads" that seem to me to be developed throughout John as a whole. Each one will be introduced by a reflection on a particular aspect of life that may both motivate and challenge us. It should be emphasized right away that these threads are not entirely separate. Overall, in John, we find them woven together into a rich tapestry that gives a distinctive texture to the text as it develops but, thematically speaking, I think they are also fairly distinctive.

In practice this means that the same chapter and verse reference may come up more than once, with a slightly different bearing in different chapters, and the interconnectedness will become clearer as the reflections on the various threads develop. We should also note that there is already a fair amount of repetition and reinforcement in John, including for instance occasional reminders simply of who people are and what they have previously done. To note just a few examples of this, compare John 11:2 and 12:3; John 3:1-2 and 19:39; John 11:49-50 and 18:14; John 13:23-25 and 21:20. Where verses, or sections of verses, are quoted verbatim, as they often will be, the translation used is the NRSV Anglicized Edition unless it is stated that a particular point is being made regarding the Greek text. It may well be helpful for readers to have a copy of the gospel to hand as they work their way through what follows.

The principal aim of this book is to do appropriate justice to the depth of John overall, while hopefully communicating my own intrigue and providing some food for thought of relevance to the reader's journey and personal adherence to the Christian faith. It is hoped that it will bring out something of the transformative potential of John to many of the bigger questions of life and faith. Overall, however, if it says at least something helpful to the reader that may not have been considered before, and perhaps more than one thing, then it will certainly have been worth my while writing it, especially since the sparking of a new idea, new connection, or fresh perspective can often be a great catalyst in the ongoing development of a journey of faith.

Chapter 1

Holistic Overview

*An End in the Beginning
and a Beginning in the End*

BIG HISTORY

One of the notable features of living in the modern world is the utter vastness of the sense of history available to us. By this I mean not just the entirety of human history, which is itself much longer than was thought by many previous generations, but the history of the entire universe—cosmic history. This is explored, among many other places, in an aptly named book, *Big History: Between Nothing and Everything*, published back in 2014, which looks at the evidence we now have available for the discernment of several critical stages and turning points in cosmic history, and especially those necessary for the emergence and subsequent development of life and civilization. One of the authors, David Christian, has subsequently produced a further volume entitled *Origin Story: A Big History of Everything*, along similar lines. Furthermore, in the run up to the start of the new millennium, while I was an A-level student studying among other things maths and physics, I remember reading the impressive book by John Barrow and Frank Tipler entitled *The Anthropic Cosmological Principle*, which examines

The Horizon of Faith

some of the remarkable, fine-tuned "coincidences" that needed to be what they were in order for it even to be possible on principle for life as we know it to occur in this universe. It is certainly the book that confirmed my first-degree-subject choice of physics.

It is a very deep privilege I think to live in an age in which we can read these and many other books that reflect the deeply intriguing background to our present context of existence. We are now able to appreciate far more about the unfolding and complex set of interrelating conditions necessary for the universe to acquire life, to acquire a means of being able to *observe* the same universe, and to become conscious of how specific and finely-honed the requirements for this remarkable feat actually are. History is big and it is deep, there are many layers to it, and each one contributes something to the texture and impression of the final canvas, which, in an absolute sense, we have yet to reach. This realization should encourage us to seek the bigger picture, the fuller perspective, and one of the things that I find draws my attention to John especially is that it seems consistently to draw attention to a bigger picture and to the basis for a fuller insight. Not only that, but it does so despite being written at a time when people would not have had the faintest idea about any of the scientific details mentioned in the many books that have now been written on the subject of the history of the universe and of the earth.

John both begins and ends on a "bigger picture" note. We hear first those famous words, "In the beginning was the Word," or the *Logos* in the Greek text (1:1),[1] the great undergirding and overarching principle both *of* and *for* everything that was to be created, and of everything to follow and unfold therefrom. Then, in the final, equally dramatic verse, we hear that there were "many other things that Jesus did" (21:25), remembering that he did them specifically as the Word made flesh (1:14). Such things have already been noted as "not written in this book" (20:30) but they nonetheless remain of relevance to what the gospel explicitly provides as the basis for a belief from which far *more* can unfold (20:31). The

---

1. All references to the wording of the Greek text are taken from Aland et al., *Novum Testamentum Graece*.

dramatic part comes in full when we then hear that the writer supposes that the entire world, *kosmos* in the Greek, would not suffice to contain the books that would need to be written *if* all things that had ever happened, or for that matter might *yet* happen, through Christ, through the *Logos*, and through the *Logos made flesh* in particular, were to be explicitly written down (21:25).

I use the Greek word, *Logos*, here because it covers a wider conceptual span than can realistically be captured by the translation "Word." The scope of the term *Logos* in this case encompasses anything and everything involved in the proper expression or communication of an idea, principle, intention, or similar, and not just through words. This even includes the principle of internal communication to oneself, through calculating or reckoning.[2] This hopefully gives a sense of the depth already being hinted at in the opening and closing verses of John, and a strikingly intuitive sense of depth in a world in which many other books, including those mentioned earlier, were indeed yet to be written.

Returning to the beginning, the Prologue in 1:1–18, we may notice that there are two mentions of the phrase "in the beginning" (1:1–2) and also effectively two mentions of the fact that "all things" were created through the *Logos* (1:3a), since "without him not one thing came into being" (1:3b). There is a certain emphasis here and an obvious parallel with the opening creation account in Genesis 1, which, among other possible implications, means that when we come to the great transition by which "the Word became flesh and lived among us" (expressed as *eskēnōsen* in the Greek, which more directly translates as pitching tent or tabernacling among us—1:14) this is already the genesis of a new creation and new beginning to follow. A new emergence, something already containing a projected end within itself, is embedded into the initial setting, the deep beginning. When we then reach the final verse of the gospel, we find within that ending the opening of a further prospect of unfolding, a deeper opening up of the mind towards the sheer *scope* of Christ's activity, which is in some sense only just

---

2. All references to possible meanings of Greek words are taken from Liddell and Scott, *Greek-English Lexicon*.

dawning on people, and the seed of which has been firmly sown throughout the gospel. That is the reason for my choice of the title for this chapter.

WATER, WIND AND SPIRIT: A DYNAMIC ENCOUNTER

Let us first review the general framework of John, as this will set the overall scene for the reflections of subsequent chapters. From just after the end of the Prologue we immediately hear about the early, preparatory witness of John the Baptist, already pre-empted in 1:6–8. John is baptizing with *water*, which is noted three times (1:26, 31, 33) and sets the tone for the early chapters of John, in which water is a recurring theme and symbol. It occurs again at the start of chapter 2, in the famous story of the wedding at Cana at which it is turned to wine, which is in itself an enrichment of the symbol—among other things that will be mentioned later on. It is then further enriched in chapter 3, when it is explicitly set alongside mention of the Spirit as Jesus instructs Nicodemus about being born "from above . . . of water and Spirit" (3:3, 5). This involves a comparison being made between one born of the Spirit and the sense of mystery, at least where origin and destination are concerned, of the wind blowing, since "you do not know where it comes from or where it goes" (3:8). We therefore already have three references to that which is fluid, dynamic, and *in flow*: water, wind, and Spirit. These are unpredictable and not within mortal control. The question of the flesh also crops up here, which becomes far more relevant later on in the gospel, but is mentioned at this point in a rather in-passing manner: "What is born of the flesh is flesh, and what is born of the Spirit is spirit" (3:6).

In chapter 4 yet another dimension is added to the water imagery, when Jesus, having asked the Samaritan woman he encounters at Jacob's well for a drink, proceeds to inform her that he gives water by which people will never thirst again and which will be "in them a spring of water gushing up to eternal life" (4:14). This water is to be established within *fleshly* life. We may also note that there are two directions at play here. In the discussion with Nicodemus the first emphasis is on what comes down from above (3:3, reinforced in different words in 3:13) but this then develops into mention of being "lifted up" (3:14) and then the aforementioned phrase in chapter 4 refers to the gushing up of the water, with the setting in this case also being a mountain (4:20).

Next, we come to something of an overlap, during which the theme starts to develop away from that which is fluid and towards the more solid food of the bread of life. The first mention of food is when Jesus's disciples urge him, "Rabbi, eat something" (4:31) and he tells them that he has food that they "do not know about" (4:32), subsequently explaining, "My food is to do the will of him who sent me and to complete his work" (4:34, noted again in 17:4). In fact, we might already notice, in this mention of completion, a parallel with Jesus's final words on the cross, "It is finished" (19:30), on which I will say more later.

The water imagery returns, however, at the start of chapter 5, at the pool by one of the gates into Jerusalem, in which the water is periodically "stirred up" (5:7) and was obviously believed to be a source of healing. A man suffering from a debilitating long-term illness is there, who can never get to the stirred-up water in time before someone else beats him to it. Jesus simply tells him, "Stand up, take your mat and walk" (5:8), and notably on a sabbath day (5:9). The man does not need any contact with the water in the pool, since Jesus himself, as the previous chapters have made clear, gives the water that is necessary, and also the *solid ground* on which this man can walk in faith. The spring of water that Jesus speaks of establishing *within* people in the previous chapter now shows a very profound effect within a previously incapacitated body next to a very symbolic spring, not least in its location at a gate leading into Jerusalem, and on a very symbolic day, the sabbath.

The overlap between the fluid imagery and the solid food imagery then continues as we come to the famous feeding of the five thousand in chapter 6, after which Jesus notably withdraws to a mountain to be on his own because he sees that people are about to "take him by force to make him king" (6:15). Jesus is not

The Horizon of Faith

to be imposed upon by human will regarding what ought to occur, another consistent theme in John. Immediately afterwards we come to a key transition point in the turning of the narrative. We move from the emphasis on the foundational, flowing dynamics of water, wind and Spirit towards an emphasis on another aspect of foundation for the nourishment of the journey of faith—the solid food of the bread of life. This transition is marked dramatically by the walking of Jesus upon the surface of the water on the Sea of Galilee, emphasizing a solidity and a fluidity *simultaneously*, and a narrative section ending with the potent words "they wanted to take him into the boat, and immediately the boat reached the land towards which they were going" (6:21). No need to bring him off the surface of the water, because solid ground has been reached in and with him. He is calling them *to him* rather than them taking him to where they are—another Johannine theme on which much more will be said later.

Before we leave this section of the narrative, we should also note here that the "three or four miles" noted in 6:19—in the Greek, "twenty-five or thirty stadia"—is a very long way to row when it is both dark and windy (6:17–18), which adds poignancy to the encountering of Jesus walking on the stormy waters in a grand symbolic gesture of conquering the chaos. We may further consider here that the Sea of Galilee is about thirteen miles long and just over seven miles wide, so they were presumably well on the way to the center of it by the time they encountered Jesus. This makes the final verse of the narrative section all the more remarkable, since, despite the significant distance involved, they *immediately* reach the land towards which they are going. Moreover, this is also a narrative section importantly including the use of a frequently repeated Johannine phrase, "I am," which Jesus declares of himself at several points. In this case the context is the phrase, "I am, do not be afraid" (6:20, and going by the Greek version of the text at this point).

Holistic Overview

A FIRM FOUNDATION AND THE BREAD OF LIFE

The reaching of the solid ground of the boat's destination at this point in the narrative paves the way for the discourse that then follows in the remainder of chapter 6 regarding the *solid food* of the bread of life and its explicit identification with the *flesh* of Christ (6:51). The question of the flesh returns, and now in a manner causing a certain grumbling and dissatisfaction—a matter both unexpected and too close to home, as it were. While the idea of a spring of living water being within us, gushing up to eternal life, is obviously and immediately appealing, not so much, at least on first hearing, the idea of eating "the flesh of the Son of Man," as Jesus refers to himself at this point, and drinking his blood (6:52–60). This requires much more thought in terms of what is really being said and its implications, and many of the listeners do not seem to have the patience for such a demand, turning away from Jesus instead (6:66). The relevance of the flesh is not bracketed off here, as it somewhat seems to be in Jesus's earlier encounter with Nicodemus, but is now centered firmly on the flesh of Jesus himself and with the explicit suggestion that this too needs to be taken *within* us.

We may then note a brief return to the water theme after the bread of life discourse, again specifically relating to an emphasis on the Spirit, and developing the "spring of water gushing up to eternal life" theme (4:14 again) into "rivers of living water" flowing out of the believer (7:38). The implication of such rivers being connected to their mutual source in the spring might well also pre-empt in our minds the famous image of the vine and the branches that follows later (15:1–5). Furthermore, the proclamation about the rivers of living water occurs on "the last day of the festival [of Booths], the great day" (7:37), which would have been the seventh day of the festival. This festival, also known as *Sukkot* (Hebrew for "booth" or "hut" or "tabernacle"—basically a specific dwelling-place)[3] commemorates the forty years the Israelites jour-

---

3. Hebrew word meanings referenced from Davidson, *The Analytical*

neyed in the wilderness following the Exodus from Egypt, based on a command in Leviticus 23:42-43. There seems therefore to be a clear connection in John between the place of Christ and the true dwelling-place of a Promised Land, through eternal provision from the life-giving spring. This in turn points towards another form of solidity, that of the link with *history*, which is made yet firmer during the course of chapters 7 and 8 following on from the bread of life discourse—a discourse which has already seen Christ declared as the fulfilment of the meaning and purpose of Moses's ministry among the people, in relation to "the manna in the wilderness" (6:31-33, 48-51).

Chapters 7 and 8 consider the significance of historical figures such as Moses and Abraham, along with questions over the origin and coming of the Messiah. They note several ways in which the solidity that Christ is offering—indeed, which Christ himself *is*—in the *present* relates to a proper manner of interpreting and recognizing the significance of the *past*. We could equally note that although 8:1-11, concerning the woman caught in adultery, seems to be an insert that is missing in many ancient versions of the text, it also fits here in the sense that the challenge with which the Pharisees test Jesus at this point is based upon their particular understanding of what Moses commanded them to do (8:5). History, and in particular the interpretation of history, inevitably plays a key role in establishing a sense of foundation and identity, but the question of how best to appreciate the firmness of one's foundation is notably developed as John progresses.

A FRESH BEHOLDING

Having visited the question of historical relevance in chapters 7 and 8, chapter 9 turns its attention to the *fresh opening of eyes* in the here and now, to the enablement to see more clearly the present dynamic and what may be recognized as unfolding as a result. The primary and highly symbolic focus is the opening of the eyes of a

---

Hebrew and Chaldee Lexicon.

Holistic Overview

man blind from birth, emphasizing the radical newness of what is being seen and appreciated in this case. This is further highlighted by Jesus's caution, "We must do the works of him who sent me while it is day; night is coming when no one can work" (9:4), so not only is this a significantly new form of seeing, or insight, but there is a critical time window, especially as Jesus's "hour" approaches—yet another big theme in John about which more will be said later.

Given that this section of the gospel is also one that transitions from the *significance of history* towards an anticipation of Christ's passion, his hour and the *future transformation* that this will bring, it is also fitting that the man in question's parents become involved. First, this occurs as a question from the disciples regarding whether the blindness is to do with the man's own transgression or parental transgression, both of which Jesus denies (9:2–3). Second, the parents are involved as a witness to the Jewish authorities that the man in question was in fact born blind and is indeed their son, but to which they reply, "Ask him; he is of age" (9:18–21). The man who momentarily stands as the dominant witness and symbol of a new seeing, brought *to* light by Christ *as* the light, is not only able to see for himself but also to speak for himself. What Christ brings into effect here is *greater* than the links with the past as either the disciples or the Pharisees are first inclined to view them. The idea of that which is "greater" is found frequently in John, as will be explored more fully in chapter 5 as the last of the five threads I will consider here.

Chapter 10 then sees Christ being explicit about the *threshold* to which those engaging with his words have been brought, to the door or gate into a new domain, and a door or gate with which Christ personally identifies (10:7–9). In chapter 11 we have the subsequent foreshadowing of the resurrection in the raising of Lazarus and the first signs of preparation for Christ's approaching suffering and death, especially in the anointing of Jesus's feet at the start of chapter 12. This is then immediately followed by John's account of the entry into Jerusalem, and the passion narrative begins in chapter 13. Unlike the other gospels, John's account contains a

The Horizon of Faith

long section from chapters 14 to 17 during which—again, among other things—the nature of Christ's peace, his relation to the Father, and the significance of this for his relation to his disciples gets fleshed out, not least in the early mention of the "place" that would be prepared for the disciples (14:2–3).

The thick of the passion narrative then begins from the start of chapter 18, with its obvious focus on the material and symbolic circumstances of Christ's trial and crucifixion. Then, post-resurrection, we find both the *breathing of the Spirit* on the disciples (20:22) and the *water* imagery returning one final time (21:1–8). Having decided to go fishing, Peter, and the others who have accompanied him, have been directed by the appearance of the resurrected Christ to cast their net into the sea. On responding to this they discover, despite having previously been without any catch, that the net is full. Peter is at first naked in the boat, and actually puts some clothes *on* before jumping into the water and swimming across to meet the risen Christ on the shore, with the others following behind him in the boat. On this occasion they are notably "not far from the land, only about a hundred yards ["two hundred cubits" in the Greek]" (21:7–8). This is in something of a contrast to the much greater distance mentioned earlier in 6:19. Again, more will be said on this episode later.

For the moment, however, let us just consider the very broad brushstrokes of the layout as so far described, involving both the dynamics of the flowing imagery of water, wind and Spirit, upon which much is in fact *grounded*, and the solidity of the food that Christ gives and of the land to which he brings us. This overall framework incorporates history and delves into its true roots in terms of its interpretation and its relevance to what is being encountered in the present in Christ, while simultaneously pointing towards a prospective future and a particular form of place that is being prepared for us. This projection is both in one sense *reached* and, in another sense, *opened up* for further exploration in the resurrection, in the unfolding of what this will really involve. It culminates in those very impactful final words regarding the insufficiency of "the world" for containment, and thereby carries an implicit message concerning our present sense of situatedness, or placed-ness.

This throws open not just a cosmic vision but a supra-cosmic vision, and one that I think should complement the vast extent of what we have now discerned about cosmic history and, for that matter, the many interesting questions about its possible future. Overall, the life of Jesus as presented in John, a life which *alone* can contain the dynamism and unpredictability suggested in relation to the water, the wind, and the Spirit, encompasses our life. At the same time, however, something of the very meaningful *fleshly* significance of that life is also to be taken and received within us.

THE SEVEN SIGNS AND THE "I AM" SAYINGS

Two other aspects of the overall layout of John, in a more formal sense, ought also to be noted or remembered at this point. The first of these is the seven signs performed by Jesus as key landmarks in the development of the first half of the gospel. These are as follows:

1. First sign, the wedding at Cana, where the water is turned into wine (2:1–12)
2. Second sign, also initiated at Cana but having its effect in Capernaum, the healing of the son of a royal official (4:46–54)
3. Third sign, the healing of the paralyzed man by the pool by the Sheep Gate entering Jerusalem, on the Sabbath (5:1–9)
4. Fourth sign, the feeding of the five thousand (6:1–14)
5. Fifth sign, Jesus walking on the water (6:16–21)
6. Sixth sign, the opening of the eyes of the man born blind (9:1–7)
7. Seventh sign, raising of Lazarus from the dead (11:1–44)

It may be noteworthy here that the first four signs involve Jesus pre-empting what he is about to do with some form of question or challenge to someone: "Woman, what concern is that to you and to me? My hour has not yet come" (2:4); "Unless you see signs and wonders you will not believe" (4:48); "Do you want to be made well?" (5:6); "Where are we to buy bread for these people to eat?" (6:5). The fifth sign is then accompanied by the reassuring words "It is I ["I am" in the Greek]; do not be afraid" (6:20), with the stormy weather being in itself a challenge, and in the final two signs it is suggested that the person to be healed or raised is in the state they are in specifically in order that God's glory may be revealed as a result (9:3; 11:4). In terms of challenge posed, we might say that the challenge in the sixth sign is in the command "Go, wash in the pool of Siloam" (9:7), which the man has to find before his eyes are opened, and in the seventh sign it lies in the fact that Jesus deliberately "stayed two days longer in the place where he was" rather than go to Lazarus immediately (11:6). Not only that, but he then tests his disciples' understanding (11:9–16) and, a little while later, that of Martha, Lazarus's sister (11:25–27, 39–40). More will be said on some of these signs in what is to follow, but for now let us simply recognize that none of these signs occur without an accompanying challenge or question, or some other requirement concerning what needs to be done or understood.

The second notable feature in John to mention from the outset is the "I am" sayings, in which the Greek words *egō eimi* are used by Christ in relation to himself, either left unqualified or qualified by an accompanying metaphor, such as the good shepherd for instance. In fact, we should start with an interesting subtlety of the Greek in the opening chapter, in which John the Baptist is asked who he is by the Jewish authorities. At first he replies "I am not the Messiah" (1:20, repeated in 3:28). In the Greek this is *egō ouk eimi ho Christos*. He is then asked if he is Elijah, and, despite a somewhat contrary message concerning the role that he fulfils being presented in the other gospels (Matt 11:14; 17:12–13, cf. Luke 1:17), perhaps implying that Jesus recognizes in John the Baptist something that he himself does not, John replies "I am not" (1:21a). In the Greek this is simply *ouk eimi*. Then he is asked

Holistic Overview

whether he is the prophet and he simply answers, "No" (1:21b), in the Greek now just *ou*.

At each stage a key word is dropped from the denial. Between the first and the second denial the word *egō*, "I," is dropped. The pronoun itself is still implied in the verb *eimi*, which means "I am" on its own, but the added use of *egō* is emphatic in the first denial. It is deliberately emphasized that *I* am not the Messiah—or alternatively *I* am not the Christ, the Anointed One. *John the Baptist* isn't, but the one who is coming after him is. Between the second and third denial the word *eimi* is dropped as well. So overall, the words *egō eimi* get dropped out of John's replies, and it is exactly these *same words* that will proceed to be used many times *by* the one who is the Christ *about* the one who is the Christ. This fits very well with John the Baptist's later declaration, "He must increase, but I must decrease" (3:30). That having been noted, we should now see the places where *egō eimi* is used explicitly in the Greek text in this manner, with my own italicizing of *I am* throughout:

1. "*I am* [he], the one who is speaking to you" (4:26). Specifically, in the context in question, this is declaring himself to be the Messiah, the Christ, the Anointed One (4:25), and Jesus is speaking with the Samaritan woman he encounters at Jacob's well. Notice that both the first of John the Baptist's denials and the first instance of Jesus saying "I am" (*egō eimi*) in the Greek text are both in reference to the Messiah or, equivalently, the Christ.

2. "*I am*" (6:20), again going by the Greek text, in response to the disciples being terrified when Jesus walks towards them on the water across the dark, wind-battered lake. I have no idea whether there is anything in it at this point, but nonetheless find it interesting that the second of John the Baptist's denials is in response to the question, "Are you Elijah?" Elijah is a rather stormy character, but also the one who famously encounters the Lord at the entrance to a cave in which he has been hiding, and who recognizes this specifically in the still, small voice that comes *after* a mighty wind,

an earthquake and fire have passed by (1 Kgs 19:11–13). In the second instance in which we hear Christ declaring "*egō eimi*," the context is a voice of calm and reassurance coming out of the surrounding turbulence.

3. "*I am* the bread of life" (6:35, repeated in 6:48). Again, it is perhaps of interest here that, while the third of John the Baptist's denials was in response to the question "Are you the prophet?" Jesus, at the point of the third *egō eimi* instance, adds the remark, "It is written in the prophets, 'And they shall all be taught by God'" (6:45a). This is said in the context of describing the nature of the feeding with the bread of life, as relating to everyone "who has heard and learned from the Father" coming to Christ (6:45b).

4. "*I am* the living bread which came down from heaven" (6:51) and further identifying the bread in question with his flesh. This increases both the qualification of what Jesus is speaking about and, of course, its intensity.

5. "You will search for me, but you will not find me; and where *I am*, you cannot come" (7:34), focusing attention on the question of place, about which I will say much more in the next chapter.

6. "*I am* the light of the world" (8:12), identifying the one who will illuminate the opacity that evidently shrouds the question of where he is from and where he is going (8:13–14), remembering again the analogy made with the wind in Jesus's words to Nicodemus (3:8).

7. "*I am* from above" and "*I am* not of this world" (8:23), with a slightly different ordering of the Greek words but nonetheless expanding the previous theme further, and immediately afterwards adding that "you will die in your sins unless you believe that *I am* [he]" (8:24).

8. "When you have lifted up the Son of Man, then you will realize that *I am* [he]" (8:28, referring back to 3:14–15).

Holistic Overview

9. Then comes a real crunch point when Jesus declares, "Very truly, I tell you, before Abraham was, *I am*." This really gets under the skin of the Jewish authorities, making as it does an unignorably divine declaration (8:58).

10. Then, in chapter 9, something occurs that could in one sense easily be overlooked, but in another sense is quite remarkable. The phrase "I am" (again, *egō eimi* in the Greek) is used by one who is *not* Christ (9:9), but who is nonetheless a living symbol of a new form of seeing being brought to bear *through* Christ. This is the man born blind on whose eyes Jesus rubs mud and sends him to wash in the pool of Siloam, which we are told "means Sent" (9:6–7). There is a dispute over whether it is the same man who can now see as used to sit and beg, with some saying, "It is he" and others saying it is just "someone like him" (9:8–9a). In the midst of this the man himself declares, "I am [the man]" (9:9b, going by the Greek text). There is perhaps a beautiful implication here that something of Christ is being shared with this man, and especially in what he stands for symbolically in this context. Is he "just him" or is he somewhat transformed, either in the view of others or in his own view? There is a possibly very rich implication in this passage, and we might note that the opening verse of chapter 9 emphasizes that *Jesus specifically* was the one who noticed this man (9:1). Moreover, once the authorities drive him, the man born blind who can now see, out of their midst, Jesus *finds him* again, asks him if he believes in the Son of Man, and then tells him that "the one speaking with you is he" (9:35–37).

11. "*I am* the gate for the sheep" (10:7, repeated in 10:9), drawing attention to the opening of the way to the place still beyond the comprehension or imagination of his audience.

12. "*I am* the good shepherd" (10:11, repeated in 10:14), emphasizing a means of accompaniment and guidance to and through the gate and beyond.

13. "*I am* the resurrection and the life" (11:25), which Jesus says to Martha just before he raises Lazarus from the dead, now also pointing to that aspect of the way and the place that endures beyond death.

14. Christ says that "where *I am*, there will my servant be also" (12:26), now explicitly pointing to the idea that we *can* come to where Christ is, in a certain contrast to 7:34.

15. "*I am* [he]" (13:19), another use of the phrase *egō eimi* on its own, this time in the context of Christ forecasting his imminent betrayal, the fulfilment of the scripture pointing towards it, and the setting of an example that he, as the master of the servants and the sender of the messengers, is giving to the disciples.

16. Christ assures the disciples that "where *I am*, there you may be also" (14:3), which reinforces 12:26 and this time is given in the context of Christ having just declared explicitly that he will go ahead of the disciples to prepare a place for them.

17. "*I am* the way, and the truth, and the life" (14:6), which now completes two previous "I am" sayings, since Christ is the opening of the way (the gate), the guider along the way (the good shepherd), and now the way itself, as well as the life according to which the way is always oriented.

18. "*I am* the true vine, and my Father is the vine-grower" (15:1) and, a few verses later, "*I am* the vine, you are the branches" (15:5), now being more explicit about the nature of the disciples' participation in what Christ is offering them and preparing for them.

19. "Father, I desire that those also, whom you have given me, may be with me where *I am*" (17:24), now reemphasizing 12:26 and 14:3 in the context of an explicit conversing with the Father who sent him into the world.

20. "*I am* [he]" (18:5, repeated in 18:8), just the words *egō eimi* once again, this time just after Jesus has asked those who have come to arrest him, "For whom are you looking?" On

the first hearing of these words, those to whom they are said step back and fall to the ground (18:6). There follows from this point the heat of the passion narrative, the great demonstration that would cause all these "I am" moments to be preserved for posterity. Interestingly, just as the "I am" sayings are subtly introduced by the declining denials of John the Baptist and the intriguing wordplay in the Greek, this final explicit use of *egō eimi* by Christ in relation to Christ is very soon after followed by Peter's infamous three denials of being a disciple of Jesus, without any wordplay for none is necessary. Instead, Jesus's particular aloneness and uniqueness is emphasized, being about to prove and accomplish what he, and he *alone*, could do.

21. Just for the sake of completion, there is arguably one more *egō eimi* occurrence, but in a rather different format to the others. It is a textual variant, not appearing in all sources, and occurs when Pilate says to Jesus, "So you are a king?" just after Jesus has spoken about his kingdom not being worldly in its nature. Jesus replies, "*You say* that I am a king" (my italics, 18:37). Just moments before his death the legacy of those powerful words is placed in the hands of Pilate, who tries to release Jesus (19:12) but can find no practical means of doing so, not least as Jesus falls silent before him when he asks, "Where are you from?" (19:9). Instead, he has a sign written in Latin, Greek and Hebrew declaring Christ as "The King of the Jews," and telling the complaining chief priests, "What I have written I have written" (19:19–22). Furthermore, the tense used here in the Greek is one normally used to indicate a completed action that has a present and enduring effect.

These particular occurrences of the words "I am" in the Greek mark some key moments of development in John. This initial chapter, the first thread of our exploration here, has been intended simply as a broad overview of some salient features of the flow and layout of John as a whole, but it hopefully gives a feel of some progressive sense of *opening up*, certain aspects of which are expressed in themes that are quite particular to John and to what I would call the Johannine idiom. Further threads involved in this opening up will be reflected upon in the four chapters that follow.

A NEWLY OPENED HORIZON

Just to end this chapter on a similar tone to the one on which it began, however, the opening up continues even after the gospel itself ends, as the final verse about the world not sufficing to contain the necessary books so beautifully hints. We may well reflect on how much we have been able to learn and discern, especially over the last hundred years or so, about what was necessary just to open up the very possibility of organic life in this cosmos in the first place, let alone for it to be sustained long enough to become conscious of itself, of its place, of its sense of questioning, wonder and searching, and above all of the foundational Word, the *Logos*, through whom it and all else came into existence. For that same *Logos* to take upon himself a human form corresponding to the terms of that existence—becoming flesh and dwelling or tabernacling among us—is as profound a claim concerning a new beginning and a new place of fulfilment as it is possible to get. That context cannot fully be comprehended by us, but it must remain viewed in some respect *as a whole* for the true wonder and immensity involved properly to dawn upon us. As John presents it, we discover a newly opened *horizon* of faith in Christ—the reason for the title of this book.

Just before moving into the more particular thread of the next chapter—the question of "place" with respect to Christ—it is as well to remind ourselves quickly that other general themes of John include the importance of being *sent* for a particular purpose and the importance of proper testimony and its acceptance. This is worth bearing in mind in what follows.

Chapter 2

An Orientation Towards God's Dwelling Among Us

Calling, Inviting and Apportioning

WHAT ARE WE ACTUALLY SEEKING?

Imagine somebody asked you what you most wanted from life, what you would *most seek*, especially if you could be guaranteed that you would have time to see it come to fruition. How easy would you find it to say for certain what that would be? Speaking personally—and I would imagine that the same would hold for many if not most of us—I would say that this question would need some significant time and thought before reaching a proper and responsible conclusion. How often do we really ask ourselves, honestly, what it is that we truly *most* desire, or want to see achieved, and why?

Some of the most remarkable and inspiring stories have indeed been the result of people coming to a relatively early and firm conclusion as to what they wanted to achieve in life, rather than just saying something like, "Well, I don't know really, I suppose just to feel that I have lived well and been a good person and that others would also recognize that." Equally, however, one might well point out that *not* everyone who has decided firmly what they

The Horizon of Faith

most want to achieve from a fairly young age has necessary gone on to achieve it. Moreover, a firm and determined conviction does not necessarily lead someone to do good or to be of help to others. Convictions, however firm, can be distorted or misguided. It is perfectly possible to have achieved what in one sense is a major success story, in terms of realizing a certain goal from unlikely beginnings, while in another sense being mainly self-serving and perhaps even having done others significant harm along the way.

In any event, there is clearly a big difference between asking someone, or asking oneself, what is most desired in terms of a life *goal* or *achievement*, and asking instead what one might most wish to seek, discern, unveil, and discover about the reality in which they are a participant. In other words, what *truth* or *insight* are we most seeking regarding our place in the scheme of things? That is something that will inevitably *develop* as we learn how better to ask the right questions, or the most helpful questions. In John it is very interesting that Christ's first words to the two disciples who leave John the Baptist in order to follow him are, "What are you looking for?" (1:38a). He turns back towards them in order to say this, having already, and very symbolically, gone on ahead of them. We should also bear in mind, given that there are two of them, that the question is posed in the plural. Regardless of individual differences in possible answers to this question, an answer is asked of them *together*.[1] They need to find a sense of seeking that they share.

Given the culture of the time, and especially given the great depth of meaning inherent in the word *shalom*—translated as peace, but something far deeper-rooted simply than an absence of obvious or overt conflict—it is reasonable to suppose that finding a place of deep peace and sense of wellbeing may be a good first candidate for a response to this question. This might further involve a sabbath-related bearing, entering into a sense of God's rest (cf.

---

1. Given that fish often represent people in the gospels—those who are fished by Christ and through his disciples—the fact that things begin in this case with two disciples, the minimum number required for *sharing* something, may also have an interesting parallel in the fact that there are specifically two fish mentioned later on in the account of the feeding of the five thousand (6:9).

Ps 95:6–11; Heb 4:1–11). The disciples' answer to Jesus's question is intriguing in this respect, since they do not respond either with a list of items or with one specific "what" as such. Rather, they respond with another *question*, and in this case it is a *where* question. They ask, "Rabbi..., where are you staying?" (1:38b). The form of address, "Rabbi," already suggests that the anticipation is to *learn* from him, and they relate this anticipation in some manner to his place of dwelling, a place in which a deeper sense of learning, of hope, and of rest might be sought.

The Rabbi in question's response then seems to be consonant with this way of thinking, and issues both an *invitation* and a *challenge* to a journey towards such rest in him. It does so in the often-quoted words, "Come and see" (1:39). The fact that, later in the same verse, we are told that "they remained with him that day," and that it was around the tenth hour, in the Greek text, that this occurred, might possibly carry connotations regarding the idea of sabbath preparation. This is speculation to a certain extent, but it is a concept that certainly reoccurs later in the gospel, finding its culmination just after Jesus's last words on the cross (19:30–31), and it gives weight to the possibility of a sabbath-related or resting-place-directed tone in which the disciples' shared response to Jesus's question is presented.

Overall, John makes considerable reference to the question of the place or the where-ness of Christ, especially in terms of origin and destination. The world may indeed struggle with the sense of where-ness that the gospel highlights, and the seed of this tension—a *creative* tension if beheld in the proper spirit—is already sown in the Prologue in the words, "He was in the world, and the world came into being through him; yet the world did not know him" (1:10). Here we have two distinctive orientational senses, *in* and *through*, which may not at first seem to be immediately compatible. On the one hand, the creation comes into being *through* him and is likewise renewed *in* him; on the other hand, he is *in* the creation and journeys *through* it in the Incarnation, which is already pointed towards "in the beginning." This, yet again, needs some thinking about. The most accessible analogy by which we can appreciate both being simultaneously true is perhaps that of the author of a novel including themself as a character within the novel, who in turn effects the crucial turn of the story in question, and this analogy will indeed be revisited later on.

At the very least, the obviously creative tension between the different senses of "through" and "in" with respect to Christ and the creation—or even "the world," as we hear mentioned repeatedly in John—adds great power to those immortal words concerning the *Logos* becoming flesh and pitching his tent or tabernacling among us (1:14). This dynamic, tabernacling theme is subsequently picked up again when Jesus asks the two disciples who follow him what it is that they are seeking, and meets with that telling reply asking in turn *where* he is staying. The dynamic response, "Come and see," then sets the scene for the particular idiom we find in John. Coming, following and consequently *seeing* are three very major themes throughout John, hence the early emphasis on the Word, the *Logos*, as the "light" and the "true light" (1:4-5, 7-9).

THE SPREADING OF THE WORD AND THE QUESTION OF CHRIST'S "PLACE"

The act of calling and inviting quickly starts spreading through a network of relations. Andrew finds his brother Simon (1:40-41) and then Philip, being called in Galilee a couple of verses later (1:43), goes and finds another disciple, Nathanael (1:45a). There is a notable diversity in the forms of recognition made among the early, named followers of Christ in John, and we will see in what follows that, more generally in this gospel, some people are allowed to see, know and do some things while others are not. Andrew announces to Simon that they "have found the Messiah" (1:41). John the Baptist testifies "that this is the Son of God" (1:34, noting that some textual variants say "God's chosen one"), and he also declares that Jesus is "the Lamb of God" (1:29, repeated in 1:36). Philip tells Nathanael that they "have found him about whom Moses in the law and also the prophets wrote, Jesus son of Joseph from Nazareth" (1:45b). Nathanael then declares shortly afterwards, "Rabbi, you are the Son of God! You are the King of Israel!" (1:49).

It might seem at first as if John is simply trying to include as many different titles and aspects to describe Jesus as possible—a Christology that is not just high but also multi-aspect—and Jesus himself adds the title "the Son of Man" at the end of the opening chapter (1:51). Each title lends a slightly different dimension or angle of approach to the question of *his place, his role, his origin*, and *his motioning to complete* that for which he is sent. We can of course add to this the many aforementioned "I am" sayings that follow from Jesus, some with qualifying statements or descriptions attached to them and others very potently left unqualified, and by all of which Jesus speaks about himself and witnesses to his being sent by the Father.

Equally, we will see later that there is a pattern extending further into the gospel, in which different people are granted very specific perspectives, questions, capacities, roles, and forms of recognition at key points. First, however, we should concentrate on what John has to say about the nature of Christ's place, the question of his *where-ness*. I say where-ness rather than whereabouts because the latter would suggest a rather more banal sense of place, as a basic and familiar form of location in space, which is definitely not what John is driving at.

Before looking at the various references as they develop throughout the gospel, let us first think further about the two key aspects of Christ's first encounter with the two disciples of whom he asks, "What are you seeking?" There is the place-related question, "Where are you staying?" and the response, "Come and see." Both are phrases we find *repeated* later in the gospel. The first time is when, just a few verses later, the location of Nazareth is mentioned by Philip, to which Nathanael responds by asking if "anything good" can originate from Nazareth, which does not get any clearly explicit, prophetic mention in the Old Testament—though the suggestion of implicit reference remains possible.

Philip, who wasn't even one of the two disciples to whom Jesus asked his opening question, replies, "Come and see" (1:46). Immediately after this we encounter another place-related question, when Nathanael asks Jesus, "Where did you come to know me?" (1:48), which leads to Jesus's famous mention of the phrase "under the fig tree"—a place of waiting, expecting and yearning, specifically with respect to the coming of the Messiah, and probably also a place of study, especially of the scriptures.[2] All-in-all, this is definitely a location strongly associated with *seeking*, echoing Jesus's opening question to the first two disciples who follow him. In Nathanael's case, this recognition on Jesus's part, seeing him under the fig tree, occurred even before Philip called him, which lends further thrust to the statement. It emphasizes that *Jesus's seeing* takes primacy, and it might also be worth noting that a mention of sitting under a fig tree in Micah 4:4 also suggests an association between this particular location and a sense of confident peace.

As a brief digression here, another occasion on which we find a repeat of this juxtaposition—a where-related question followed by the response, "Come and see"—occurs at the scene of the raising of Lazarus from the dead, when Jesus himself asks the where question. In this case it is a where-abouts question, "Where have you laid him?" Rather than give the basic answer, such as pointing to or detailing the location of the tomb, they reply instead, "Lord, come and see" (11:34). This is immediately followed by the mention that, "Jesus began to weep" (11:35) and, in comparison with the context of chapter 1, the irony alone is surely enough to move him to tears. Having originally been asked about where he was staying—more broadly pointing to the nature of his dwelling among us—and responded, "Come and see" by way of a *dynamic invitation to a fullness of life*, his own question about Lazarus now meets with a request to him to "come and see" the *static resting*

---

2. Here there are some interesting references, not least if one searches online with the phrase "under the fig tree." Three distinctive interpretations of the encounter with Nathanael are offered online for comparison by Grondin, "What Is Nathanael and the Fig Tree About?"

An Orientation Towards God's Dwelling Among Us

place of a dead body, but one which he will, nevertheless, restore to life. I mention this deep irony early on because it gives a flavor for the sense of interconnectedness that seems to run throughout John, especially with regard to particular key themes that get developed along the way. In this case, the matter of Jesus's where-ness is one that is engaging, open, and living.

Let us now return to where we left off, at the end of the opening chapter of John. We encounter the next where-related comment subtly tucked into the opening narrative of chapter 2. In the midst of the story about the water being turned into wine at the wedding at Cana it is remarked that the steward who tasted the wine "did not know *where* it came from (though the servants who had drawn the water knew)" (my italics, 2:9). In wonder about the fact that it was also the "good wine" kept until last (2:10), the steward directs a question immediately to the bridegroom, another title that comes to be attributed to Christ himself in chapter 3 (3:29).

Next, in chapter 3, Jesus mentions in his discourse with Nicodemus that, just as one could not fathom the precise motion of the wind, being sure neither of its origin nor of its destination, so likewise is the case "with everyone who is born of the Spirit" (3:8). This highlights the theme of origin, asking "from where?" and of destiny, emphasizing the question of where someone or something is heading, and we hear a powerful resonance of this later on when Jesus refers to "the Son of Man ascending to where he was before" (6:62).

In chapter 4 Jesus then asks the Samaritan woman at the well for a drink, before telling her that, if she had known who was asking her, she would have asked him for a drink and he would have given her living water. In reply she asks Jesus, "Sir, you have no bucket, and the well is deep. *Where* do you get that living water?" (my italics, 4:11). Moreover, this is shortly followed by the where-related question of which mountain should be worshipped on (4:20)—in other words, where true praise is to be offered or where the center of gravity of liturgical life, in the broadest sense of the expression, lies. The response involves the bringing in of a new vision of worship place, based on worshipping "the Father in

The Horizon of Faith

spirit and truth" (4:23), which in effect is something of a trinitarian statement, since the Son is explicitly identified with the truth later in John (14:6). This, in turn, nicely paves the way for the developing sense of trinitarian participation that we find in John, on which I shall say more in the next chapter. It is also followed shortly afterwards by yet another mention of the phrase "come and see," when the Samaritan woman, having fittingly left her water-jar with Jesus, returns to her city and tells the people, "Come and see a man who told me everything I have ever done!" (4:28–29). The place of Christ is spreading all over, even into people's individual history.

In chapter 5 Jesus disappears into a crowd, so that the man he heals on the sabbath by the Sheep Gate in Jerusalem does not know who or where he is (5:13) until Jesus later *finds him* "in the temple" (5:14), and we should notice that this fits the Johannine idiom by which Christ primarily finds us and not vice versa. Both his seeing and his finding take precedence.

In chapter 6 Jesus asks Philip, to test him, "Where are we to buy bread for these people to eat?" knowing full well "what he was going to do," in the famous narrative of the feeding of the five thousand, and we may note that this specifically testing question by Jesus is unique to John's account (6:5–6).[3] Next, in a slight deviation from asking where, but nonetheless with a similar principle of wondering involved, those seeking Jesus after their experience of the feeding ask, "Rabbi, when did you come here?" because they have found him on the opposite side of the lake but without having seen him get into a boat (6:22–25). In between these two sections we have the account of Jesus walking on the water, but those who are asking are unaware of this. At this point they cannot really get beyond the question of where-abouts, but even this is causing intrigue. Jesus, however, tells them that the key question is the nature of their own *seeking*. He informs them, "Very truly, I tell you, you are looking for me, not because you saw signs, but because you ate your fill of the loaves" (6:26).

---

3. It is also in John that we hear that the food which is shared, after Christ has given thanks over it, is originally brought along by a young child (6:9).

Then, in chapter 7, Jesus's brothers want as many people as possible to see what Jesus is doing, and want him to come with them to the festival of Booths, also called the festival of Tabernacles. Having first told his brothers that he is not going to the festival he then goes "in secret," and once again we see the Jesus who is not to be imposed upon. Even an awareness of his whereabouts is only to be discovered when the time and place is right, in this case in the temple in "the middle of the festival" (7:8–14). We then hear something of a reverse sentiment a little later on, when some of the people suggest that they *do* know where Jesus is from, but that "when the Messiah comes, no one will know where he is from," to which Jesus responds by pointing out that, although they know in an earthly sense where he is from, they do not know the where-ness that places him in relation to the one who sent him, with whom he has come and not on his own (7:27–29). This statement continues the developing trinitarian vibes that we encounter in John and re-echoes statements already heard in the Prologue regarding the Word being "with" God as well as being God, and the same Word also becoming flesh and tabernacling among us. It is especially fitting therefore that John references the festival of Tabernacles in this manner.

This also paves the way for the first mention of the idea that, after "a little while longer" Christ would return to the one who sent him and that people will search for him without finding him. Christ declares that they will not be able to come where he is, and the famous Johannine words "I am" are used in the Greek text at this point (7:33–34). This leads to a follow-on question, "Where does this man intend to go that we will not find him? . . . What does he mean by saying, 'You will search for me and you will not find me' and, 'Where I am, you cannot come'?" (7:35–36). Jumping ahead here slightly, because it is relevant to do so at this point, a second mention of this idea is made to the disciples who are with Jesus at the supper at which he washes their feet. Jesus says to them, "Little children, I am with you only a little longer. You will look for me; and as I said to the Jews so now I say to you, 'Where I am going, you cannot come'" (13:33). Interestingly, this is followed just a few verses later by a third mention of the same idea, when Jesus says, "Where I am going, you cannot follow me now; but you will follow afterwards" (13:36), and *in between* these two statements we find the giving of the new commandment to love each other just as Christ has loved us (13:34–35).

This comes at something of a turning point, since much of the second half of chapter 13 has been about a troubling of spirit and the foretelling of betrayal and denial (13:21, 26–27, 37–38), but then, just after the giving of the new commandment, we enter chapter 14 with the highly comforting and encouraging words, "Do not let your hearts be troubled" (14:1, repeated in 14:27 in relation to Christ's giving of peace, on which I will say more later on). This is followed immediately by mention of Christ going ahead of the disciples to "prepare a place" for them (14:2–3). The opening to the place of rest is becoming clearer and more explicit as events unfold.

More will be said on this below, but for the moment let us return to where we left off in chapter 7. Questions of where-ness are having both divisive and ripple effects in John. One overt division becomes very obvious in chapter 7 when it is said, "Surely the Messiah does not come from Galilee, does he?" This is followed by the remark that he ought to come from Bethlehem on account of Davidic ancestry, and the explicit division caused in the crowd is highlighted in the following verse (7:41–43, with a similar tension repeated in 7:52). Moreover, the Bethlehem statement strongly contrasts with the previous statement that no one would know where the Messiah is from (7:27), unless two different conceptions of place are consciously being held alongside one another. That is unlikely at this point, given the lack of insight that seems to prevail in response to Jesus's words, but equally John is curiously silent on the connection between Christ and Bethlehem that we are familiar with from Matthew and Luke.

There is then a further development of the where-ness and where-abouts theme in chapter 8, first, somewhat interestingly, within the section considered to be an insert which is missing in most ancient versions of the text, in which Jesus asks the woman

An Orientation Towards God's Dwelling Among Us

who had been caught in adultery, "Woman, where are they? Has no one condemned you?" (8:10). Her accusers have indeed had to *change their position* in more ways than one in response to the challenge, "Let anyone among you who is without sin be the first to throw a stone" (8:7). Christ's place has a notable effect on that of others in this case, not least as they all go off in turn, leaving Jesus and the woman alone (8:9).

Next, when the Pharisees accuse Jesus of testifying on his own behalf, therefore supposedly invalidating his testimony, Jesus responds by saying that, even if he does testify on his own behalf, it "is valid because I know where I have come from and where I am going," along with the suggestion that, because they do *not* know this, they only "judge by human standards," or, in the Greek text, "according to the flesh" (8:13-15). The questioning of the Pharisees then expands to asking explicitly, "Where is your Father?" (8:19) and Jesus repeats the message that he is "going away" and that they will search for him unsuccessfully without being able to come where he is going (8:21). It is eventually upon emphasizing *explicitly* that his origin is not worldly that they move from asking where-related questions to asking directly, "Who are you?" (8:23-25, repeated in 8:53).

When Jesus then has to evade having stones thrown at him, we hear another rather telling line, and especially so in a gospel of high Christology that contains very early mention of the new temple that would be Jesus's body (2:18-21, more on which later on). We are told that "Jesus hid himself and went out of the temple" (8:59). The temple was, among other things, a means of appreciating and representing the where-ness of God and the presence of God's sustaining activity in creation, of which the temple was effectively a microcosm.[4] To combine the idea of a certain *hiddenness* to Jesus—especially where an understanding of his origin, his personhood, and the true depth of his mission and purpose were concerned—with the idea of his *leaving* the physically visible temple whose place his questioners considered themselves to be

---

4. A quite beautiful description of this can be found, as written from a Jewish perspective, in Levenson, *Sinai and Zion*, 137-145.

familiar with, but later to reveal a new temple in his body, is therefore very fitting. Even if, at first, the remark seems entirely matter of fact, there is a sense of developing subtlety regarding what those questioning and accusing him *cannot* see.

Chapter 9 continues the where-abouts/where-ness theme, when the man born blind, who has just had his eyes opened, is asked where the one who opened his eyes is, to which he too replies "I do not know" (9:12). This is further echoed by the Pharisees when they quiz him about Jesus (9:29), to which the man in turn replies, "Here is an astonishing thing! You do not know where he comes from, and yet he opened my eyes" (9:30). There is a part of me that wants to place a particular emphasis here, namely that *they*, the Pharisees, do not know where Jesus comes from, and yet he opened *his*, the man born blind's eyes. This emphasis seems somewhat merited, since the man in question suddenly and rather unexpectedly starts to presume to teach the Pharisees, saying, "We know that God does not listen to sinners, but he does listen to one who worships him and obeys his will. Never since the world begun has it been heard that anyone opened the eyes of a person born blind. If this man were not from God, he could do nothing" (9:31–33). Needless to say, the authorities do not take kindly to this presumption to teach them, and drive him out as well (9:34).

We then hear speculation about where Jesus surely *won't* be, as by this point authority has formally been given for his arrest. People are saying, "Surely he will not come to the festival, will he?" (11:56–57). The Greek wording of the question also seems strongly to negate the mere possibility of him doing so, and Christ's approaching passion would indeed surprise everyone in one way or another. Again, Christ's initiative and say-so prevail over all else.

Shortly afterwards there follows a notable combination of two Johannine themes, when a where-related statement directly coincides with a use of the words *egō eimi*, and in a context that relates to servants of Christ as well as to Christ himself. Namely, Christ declares, "Whoever serves me must follow me, and where I am, there will my servant be also" (12:26). This is what is subsequently emphasized in chapter 14 with regard to the preparing

An Orientation Towards God's Dwelling Among Us

of a place, specifically that "if I go and prepare a place for you, I will come again and will take you to myself, so that where I am, there you may be also" (14:3). This is followed, however, by the dissention-provoking statement that the disciples somehow know at least "the way" even if they do not know "the place" (14:4). Thomas then asks how they can "know the way" if they do not know the final destination (14:5), which is, effectively, then stated by Jesus as being the Father in whose "house" the dwelling-place is prepared. In this sense, the Son *becomes* the house in question (14:6, held in conjunction with 14:2). Interestingly, no one at this point asks a direct question about where he is going, on which Jesus himself subsequently comments (16:5). The nature of the dynamic, and of the relation between Christ and his followers, gradually develops and unfolds further.

Moving ahead now to chapter 17, we hear Christ addressing the Father directly, including the reinforcing sentence, "Father, I desire that those also, whom you have given me, may be with me where I am, to see my glory, which you have given me because you loved me before the foundation of the world" (17:24). Once again this combines the phrase "I am" with a deeply meaningful mention of where-ness, in this case related back to the pre-world dynamic found in the opening verses of the Prologue. Given that the Prologue clearly looks back to the creation account in Genesis 1, there follows what in one sense is a dramatic shift but in another sense is highly appropriate. The main passion narrative, beginning at the start of chapter 18, notably starts with reference to "a place where there was a garden" (18:1), and the concept of a garden, such as that of Eden, often played a role in representing on earth a heavenly glory, just as the temple was to house a sanctuary that was "a sketch and shadow of the heavenly one" (Heb 8:5).

In Eden, of course, the garden is also a setting that sees a rebellion, a disobedience, based on a deceitful misconception regarding the true relation between divinity and humanity (Gen 3:4–5). The fruit of the tree of knowledge being taken *out of its proper place* is a very fitting way of representing this, along with the subsequent realization of a vulnerable nakedness and a need for a self-constructed covering (Gen 3:7). In Genesis this event is also followed by a very telling where-related question, when the LORD God calls to the man and asks, "Where are you?" (Gen 3:9). This question can hardly be considered as being for God's benefit, since God presumably knows perfectly well. The where-ness question seems here to be more broadly spiritual or existential in its nature, and for humanity's attention and benefit. What sense of where-ness, what deeper sense of orientation has been lost as a result of the disobedience? There needs to be some internal realization of what has happened to and within us, prompted by the question, "Who told you that you were naked?" (Gen 3:11). Now in a state of existential nomadicism cast outside of Eden, humanity perceives a lingering echo of incompleteness and anxious vulnerability. When the New Testament talks of a Second Adam and the new humanity in Christ (Rom 5:12-21; 1 Cor 15:45-49), it is then fitting that the where-ness question should find its proper resolution and full reconciliation also with respect to Christ, and this is something very evident in the development that we find in John.

In the early part of chapter 18 disruption once again enters the garden area, as Judas, perhaps thinking he *knew* best how to provoke Jesus to the kind of liberating action many expected of the Messiah, brings a detachment of soldiers to arrest Jesus (18:2-3). Intriguingly, Jesus comes forward towards them and asks, "For whom are you looking?" (18:4), which might remind us somewhat of his very opening question to the first disciples back in the opening chapter, "What are you looking for?" Furthermore, just as the thick of the passion narrative begins with mention of a garden, it also ends with mention of a garden, containing "a new tomb in which no one had ever been laid" (19:41). This is highly fitting given the association with the seed of a new creation in what is to follow, with Jesus having already said that "unless a grain of wheat falls into the earth and dies, it remains just a single grain; but if it dies, it bears much fruit" (12:24). Not only that, but in this new garden Mary Magdalene has the *same* question repeated to her—"For whom are you looking?"—by someone she does *not* at first recognize as Jesus, until he addresses her by name in the following

An Orientation Towards God's Dwelling Among Us

verse. Instead, she presumes that he is the gardener (20:15). In a higher sense of course Christ *is* the gardener, since he is the Second Adam, the new humanity in relation to the Eden narrative in Genesis. The links in relation to place and recognition, and to seeing and knowing, have become progressively thicker as John continues.

An especially potent where-related question then occurs just moments before the crucifixion, when a worried Pilate who has just heard that Jesus "claimed to be the Son of God" goes and asks him directly, "Where are you from?" Very poignantly at this point, the question is met with *silence* (19:7–9). This unexpected silence rather amplifies the distinctive sense of isolation and the uniqueness of Christ's place that we find in John, especially as the climax of the passion narrative is reached.

The where-abouts/where-ness references also continue after the resurrection. Mary Magdelene says to two of the disciples, "They have taken the Lord out of the tomb, and we do not know where they have laid him" (20:2), and shortly afterwards she repeats this in a more intensely personalized manner to the two angels in white who appear in the tomb (20:13b). Almost immediately after that she repeats a similar remark about the where-abouts of Jesus's body—or corpse, as she believes it at this point to be—without realizing that she is by this point speaking to Jesus directly (20:15). Moreover, "where the body of Jesus had been lying" there are the two angels, who, rather than explicitly answer the where-abouts question, ask instead simply why she is weeping (20:12–13a). We might further note that in her weeping Mary is first simply described as standing (20:11a),[5] whereas, in order subsequently and more properly to look, even through her tears, and to see something she may otherwise have missed, she needs to bend, turn, and reorient herself to begin to behold and recognize the new place of Jesus (20:11b, 14, 16).

This new sense of where-ness will take some time fully to dawn, and it is notable in this case that the two disciples who first

---

5. In an interesting contrast, we are told that the angels in the tomb are "sitting" (20:12).

ran to the tomb on hearing Mary Magdalene's report simply "returned to their homes" afterwards (20:10), in which we might hear a lingering tone of some earlier words of Christ, "each one to his home" (16:32). Yet it is out of those homes into a new sense of dwelling-place that we are to be drawn. This "drawing" is very important in John, as will be reflected on more fully later, and Christ distinctively takes the initiative in this. He also tells Mary Magdalene, "Do not hold on to me" (20:17) since he has yet to ascend to the Father who is both his and, through and in him, hers. The concept of place, dwelling and belonging is both deepened and transformed in this new life and new creation in Christ. Indeed, we may consider how the basis of our trust in the explicit declaration of 2 Corinthians 5:17—"So if anyone is in Christ, there is a new creation: everything old has passed away; see, everything has become new!"—is in effect gradually unfolded throughout John as the narrative develops.

There is then, finally, the reference to the *change* of relationship with place that occurs as one gets older, and the difference this makes for Peter in going wherever he wished when he was younger, but being taken to where he does not wish to go when he grows old, pointing ultimately towards his death, and the type of death that it would be (21:18–19). Overall, we can say that the concept of place, of belonging, of destination, and of our specific relation to the deep question of the where-ness of God is thoroughly explored in John. Having therefore considered the depth and breadth with which the concept of where-ness is explored and described in John in relation to Christ, we should now also consider how place, role, and perspective are distributed among those who encounter Jesus in the outworking of that for which he was sent as the gospel progresses. This is another notable thread in John that complements the emphasis on the *centrality* of the place of Christ.

An Orientation Towards God's Dwelling Among Us

FINDING OUR PLACES: ALLOCATION WITHIN A SHARED DISCIPLESHIP

Beginning in chapter 2 we hear of various distinctive roles at the wedding at Cana. First, Mary, the mother of Jesus, draws his attention to the fact that the wine has run out, and, even when he asks her what that has to do with either of them, she still clearly anticipates a response, saying to the servants, "Do whatever he tells you" (2:3–5). The servants are then the ones who fill the stone jars with water and then draw some of the water out, but do not actually taste it (2:7–8). The tasting is done by the chief steward, who does not know where it has come from, while the servants do (2:9). Already we see a subtle allocation of roles and places. Early in chapter 4 we then hear that it is the disciples, rather than Jesus himself, who actually perform the baptisms as people come over in greater numbers from John the Baptist to Jesus (4:1–2). Later on, in the same chapter, Jesus remarks, "One sows and another reaps," and notes that the disciples are sent to reap that for which they did not at first labor (4:37–38).

We should further consider the characters of Mary and Martha, mention of whom spans a considerable narrative section in John, effectively running from 11:1 until 12:8. The beginning and end parts of the section in question mention all of Lazarus, Mary and Martha, and where the two sisters are concerned there is an interesting pattern. In the opening verse Mary is mentioned first and Martha second (11:1) and the trouble is taken to mention that it is the *same* Mary "who anointed the Lord with perfume and wiped his feet with her hair" (11:2), which seems to suggest that this had already occurred earlier but which is in fact an event not reported explicitly in John until later, near the end of the section of the narrative involving the two sisters (12:3). Not only is it clearly considered relevant to emphasize that it is the same Mary in both cases, but it also means, regardless of the ordering of the events in reality,[6] that she is, over all, mentioned both first and last of the two

---

6. We can only speculate, but the anointing part of the narrative at the start of chapter 12 begins by referring to Lazarus as the one "he had raised from the

35

The Horizon of Faith

of them (comparing 11:1-2 and 12:2-3). Mention of her tops and tails the entire broader section of narrative, as it were.

Then, as we step towards the middle of the narrative in question, we see Martha having moments of considerable emphasis. She is mentioned first in 11:5 and Mary is then referred to only as "her sister" rather than by name, and she is mentioned first again in 11:19 and 11:20. Martha, without needing to be asked explicitly, is the one to go out first and meet Jesus, while Mary stays at home. Martha greets Jesus saying, "Lord, if you had been here, my brother would not have died," and follows it immediately with an *explicit* show of faith that "God will give you whatever you ask of him" (11:21-22). She then confidently and overtly affirms Jesus's response that Lazarus would rise again, leading in turn to another "I am" saying—"I am the resurrection and the life" (11:23-26). When asked if she believes this statement from Jesus, she then uses three *explicit* descriptions of Jesus in immediate succession, namely "the Messiah, the Son of God, the one coming into the world" (11:27). It is notable at this point that Jesus gives *no explicit response*, and, given that the next verse has Martha return home and tell Mary privately, "The Teacher is here and is calling for you" (11:28), we can *implicitly* deduce that Jesus's response was in some way to wish to involve Mary.

While Martha automatically supposes that she will be wanted or needed, without being asked explicitly, but then explicitly announces what she is thinking, Mary shows rather the opposite pattern. Mary does seem to need to be explicitly asked or invited to go to Jesus, yet, once this happens, she gets up quickly and goes out to meet Jesus, not on her own like Martha but followed instead by all who were consoling her (11:29-31). She comes to the same place as Martha went, *kneels at Jesus's feet*—the feet she will later anoint in 12:3—and repeats the same opening words as Martha uttered before her (11:32). Here, however, instead of giving a similar, explicit statement of faith like Martha, we simply hear that Jesus witnesses her and the others who were consoling her all weeping together, and this time we find a very different

---

dead," suggesting that the events of chapter 11 did indeed come first.

form of *explicit response from Jesus*. He is "greatly disturbed in spirit and deeply moved," (11:33) and we reach at this point what is effectively the center of gravity of the narrative, when Jesus asks the where question, "Where have you laid him?" This meets with the deeply ironic response, "Lord, come and see," upon which Jesus weeps (11:34-35). As I have indicated, I believe this to be a deeply significant moment in the gospel, the poignant irony of which has already been remarked upon.

Then it is Martha's turn again, responding to Jesus ordering the stone to be rolled away from Lazarus's tomb by objecting, "Lord, already there is a stench because he has been dead for four days." Here we have another explicitly expressed concern, betraying that she hasn't grasped what Jesus is doing and thereby causing Jesus to remind her explicitly of what he had said to her previously (11:39-40). The seventh sign, the raising of Lazarus, follows and then this section of narrative finishes with mention of Mary, since we are told that many of those accompanying her came to believe (11:45). In all of this we should of course remember that it is emphasized that Jesus loves all concerned (11:3, 5), but the distribution of roles and places is nonetheless quite intriguing, even rather obvious when seen in this way. Even if the distinction is connected with Martha being the elder sister, the interesting structure that this lends to the narrative in itself remains of relevant interest.

If we then include the section of narrative in 12:1-8, we hear, in consistency with the story of Mary and Martha from Luke 10:38-42, that "Martha served" (12:2) while Mary, again at Jesus's *feet* (cf. Luke 10:39), performs the highly symbolic and *implicitly* meaningful action of anointing Jesus's feet with "costly perfume," filling the whole house with its fragrance (12:3). Interestingly, this meets with explicit criticism from Judas Iscariot that the perfume should have been sold for the benefit of the needy, clarified in brackets as not being remarked out of concern for the poor but because he could then steal from the common purse (12:4-6). Jesus's reply is very fitting, saying, "Leave her alone, *so that she might keep it* for the day of my burial" (my italics, 12:7).[7] This guarding

---

7. Here I am going by the Greek text, since the NRSV translation adds

statement by Jesus seems to me rather to echo the words from Luke's account of his encounter with Mary and Martha, when he says to Martha, "Mary has chosen the better part, which will *not be taken away from her*" (my italics, Luke 10:42).

Interestingly, there is a distinct similarity between this story and a story in the other gospels in which Jesus is in the house of a leper called Simon, where a woman comes with a jar of costly ointment and pours it on Jesus's head, upon which Jesus says of her that "wherever this [or "the"] good news is proclaimed in the whole world, what she has done will be told in remembrance of her" (Matt 26:13; Mark 14:9; with a somewhat different version of the story in Luke 7:36–50). It is doubtless fitting to John's high Christology, as will be the subject of the next chapter, that it is Jesus's *feet* that are anointed, rather than his head, and no suggestion is made in John that any mortal being might presume to do so. The head, in John, may perhaps emphasize the inseparable relation to the Father—a relation that pertains to an uncontainable sense of place from a mortal perspective. More on this idea will follow later.

Let us just summarize here the sandwich-style structure of this considerable section of narrative:

(a) Mary gets the lead mention (11:1–2).

(b) Jesus, hearing about Lazarus's illness, remains where he is for two days and tests his disciples' understanding, including saying that he is glad he was not there when Lazarus died, so that they may believe, and that it is for the glory of God (11:3–16).

(c) Martha takes the lead mention and makes the first move (11:5, 17–27), including a mention of the four days that Lazarus has already been lying in the tomb and several explicit statements of faith.

---

some extra words here which it then acknowledges, in a footnote, do *not* occur in the Greek text.

(d) Mary is called over, bringing along other mourners, and takes her place at Jesus's feet. There is weeping with a general disturbance of spirit, including in Jesus himself (11:28–33).

(e) The pivotal and irony-provoking question, "Where have you laid him?" and the emotionally wrenching response, "Lord, come and see" (11:34).

(d) Repeat mention of Jesus being disturbed, including some disagreement among the onlookers about what the response to Jesus's weeping should be (11:35–38).

(c) Martha takes the lead with another explicit statement, including another mention of Lazarus being in the tomb for four days (11:39).

(b) Jesus now performs the sign itself, with the tested disciples and other onlookers as witnesses, including another mention of "the glory of God" (11:40–44).

(a) Mary gets the final mention (11:45, and again in 12:3 with a brief preceding mention of Martha serving).

There is great depth in this intriguingly structured narrative, especially when considered as a whole, involving a subtle blend of the explicit and the implicit, with the latter in particular having deep meaning, lasting consequence, and even significant irony. There is a clear sense in which the characters involved naturally find their own place in and around Christ.

Later on, beginning in chapter 13, we then hear mention of Peter in relation to another disciple, who is described as "the one whom Jesus loved." This other disciple is first mentioned as the one reclining right next to Jesus at the supper, to whom Peter gives the instruction to ask Jesus who it is who would betray him. Peter seems more distanced here, but he also seems to have a certain instructive authority (13:23–25). We subsequently hear of Peter and "another disciple"—possibly the same one as mentioned at the supper—who, because he is "known to the high priest," is able to accompany Jesus into the high priest's courtyard, while Peter at first waits outside. The other disciple then arranges for Peter to

The Horizon of Faith

be let in as well, at which point he is challenged regarding being a disciple of Jesus and, as Jesus had previously foretold (13:38), he denies that he is a disciple (18:15–17). Here Peter is also at some distance, and feeling the pressure of Jesus's foretelling regarding his denial. He repeats the denial twice a few verses later (18:25–27).

Then, just after the tomb has been found empty by Mary Magdalene, we hear that she runs to tell "Peter and the other disciple, the one whom Jesus loved," at which point they both run to the tomb, but "the other disciple" is faster than Peter, and he arrives at the scene of the resurrection mystery first . . . but he does not enter. Peter reaches the tomb second, but goes in first, eventually to be followed by the other disciple, of whom it is then first said that "he saw and believed" (20:1–8). Here there is a slight change in focus, but Peter again gets a sense of authority and now even priority in some respect.

Then the story continues in the final chapter of John, when Peter takes the initiative of announcing that he is going fishing and the other disciples follow him on what turns out, however, to be a catchless night (21:3). On encountering an at first unrecognized Jesus on the shore, "the disciple whom Jesus loved" is then the first explicitly to recognize him and declare, "It is the Lord!" Peter, however, is the first to respond to this recognition of the risen Lord on the beach by swimming across to meet him, followed by the others (21:7–8). He is, however, then subsequently challenged, "Simon son of John, do you love me more than these?" and we should note that this is despite the other disciple being described as the one whom Jesus loved. This challenge occurs no fewer than three times, inevitably recalling Peter's three denials in so doing (21:15–17).[8]

Finally, Peter specifically points out "the disciple whom Jesus loved" and says, "Lord, what about him?" This meets with the

---

8. Interestingly there is also repeated mention in John of a "charcoal fire," first just inside the high priest's courtyard at the point where Peter makes his first denial of Jesus (18:18), and second on the beach where Peter is the first to reach the risen Christ, on which the breakfast to which Jesus subsequently invites the disciples is cooking (21:9). Peter is then, very potently given the context, reminded of the denials.

reply, "If it is my will that he remain until I come, what is that to you?" (21:20–22). Regardless of any deep analysis of what is meant at this point, there certainly seems to be a hefty distinctiveness drawn in John, even among the dynamics and response of individual disciples, where the question of *place*, *role*, and *perspective* in relation to Christ is concerned. Both these two characters, Peter and the disciple whom Jesus loved, have such a place, but each is qualified differently, which may in turn remind us of Jesus's earlier words, "In my Father's house there are many dwelling-places" (14:2). Christ, however, has a clearly consistent and *defining* priority in his seeing, his finding, his calling, and his place.

OUR SENSE OF REALITY

Let us return then to the question with which this chapter began, namely, what it really is that we are most deeply seeking, individually or collectively. In the ongoing process of seeking and searching *within* the enveloping context we call our "reality," rather than merely working towards the achievement of an arbitrary goal that we have in some way extracted or abstracted *from* it, the question of *how* we perform that seeking becomes inseparable from how we come more deeply to appreciate our sense of place. We are all situated beings, and how our sense of situatedness develops can speak volumes for the nature of our perspective, the developing perception of our role—whether by us or by others—and perhaps also the depth of our appreciation of the true center of gravity of the reality in which we are asked by Christ himself what we are *most* seeking. In John, the center is clearly inseparable from the nature of Christ's place as the *Logos* made flesh. Among other things, such big questioning, mirroring the *Big History* background of the previous chapter, will have a profound effect with respect to both mental health and theological orientation. Again, John presents a very compacted narrative in which a great deal happens in a short space, but it is clear that a major developing theme involves finding a resonance between our own sense of where-abouts, in all our individual differences and distinctiveness, and the foundationally rooting matter of the where-ness of Christ, especially in his relation to the Father.

That having been said, it is now certainly time to move to consider the next big theme, that of John's high Christology and the development of a sense of God as Trinity.

Chapter 3

John's High Christology
Trinitarian Witness and Indwelling Participation

ARE WE REALLY PART OF THIS?

The previous chapter considered a particular framing of the question as to what we are most seeking deep down, whether we realize it at first or not. It did so by contemplating the matter of our place in relation to God's where-ness, and this in turn has already been seen to suggest some center of gravity to the nature of our place and the meaning of our existence, towards which we are to be drawn. This is a fitting metaphor when one considers that the Hebrew word that is normally translated as "glory" in the Hebrew Scriptures—in phrases such as "the glory of the Lord"—literally refers to a degree of weightiness.

Some might of course respond to all this by saying, "Well, that's all very well, but where is the hard evidence that I am actually part of this?" I sometimes hear people asking what is the relevance of theology, or a sermon, or even simply a particular topic of discussion to their daily lives. Reasonable though this sounds at first, I do have two big cautions about this question.

Firstly, it centers reality on a life that is presented to others as something which one "owns"—*my* daily life—which is already a big step towards centering reality on us rather than living the ec-centric, off-center life of faith that centers on God as creating, sustaining, revealing, and giving life, including new life. To center on ourselves therefore is already to impoverish the scope and the depth of theological engagement, since it at least implicitly risks suggesting that nothing theological should demand thinking about, or be considered of interest, unless the immediate benefit to oneself in the here and now is somehow made obvious. The benefit of theological thought simply for the sake of *deeper exploration* can so easily be missed here, and for that matter in any walk of life that does not, on the face of it, seem overtly accentuated in theological terms.

My second concern about the manner, and sometimes the tone, in which questions like this can get posed is that it implies that the "daily life" in question is, ordinarily, theologically passive. It suggests an expectation that relevance should be delivered to it without the kind of searching engagement suggested in many parts of the biblical witness. It is as if what is really sought is simply a useful set of answers, handed to us. It would, certainly to my mind, be much better to *empower* the daily life in question by turning the matter around and asking, instead, what is the theological relevance *of* that daily life and how can it be directed, by an inward and outward searching, to discern more about whatever deeper relevance it might hold, especially with respect to the true center of gravity of reality, the life of divinity.

That definitely seems to me to be the way advocated in John. The overall answer to the question, "Am I really part of this?"—at least in as far as it is posed by someone who really wants the answer to be positive—is a resounding "yes." However, the form of the "yes" in question is not that of a doorstep delivery by which we just stay exactly where we are, and perhaps also at first where we consider that we wish to be. Mentally and spiritually speaking at least, we must move *onwards*, and how we come to hear the affirmative "yes" will depend on how the process of seeking and following works itself out. Put slightly differently, we seek a certain onward-ness in relation to the deepest source of our existence, accompanying the where-ness question of the previous chapter, and this requires being both inwardly and outwardly aware, and searchingly engaged. It is also through this active engagement that the *way* by which we journey becomes capitalized, so to speak. It is personalized and revealed as pertaining to the centering of a new creation in the *Logos* who became flesh, having a divine personhood which, largely thanks to the trinitarian witness of John, we now call the Second Person of the Trinity.

As already noted, John has an unfailingly high Christology, but before we turn to think about the development of trinitarian witness in John, it is as well to reflect on how unique and self-sufficient John's presentation of Jesus actually is, especially when we consider the great many things in this gospel that Jesus *alone* does or knows, in addition to the signs and "I am" sayings already mentioned.

JESUS ALONE: THE PRIMACY AND UNIQUENESS OF CHRIST

Right from the outset in John it is only through the Word, the *Logos*, that things are created, even to the point of emphasizing that "without him not one thing came into being" (1:3). Life is to be found in him specifically, who is also "the light of all people" (1:4), and the darkness cannot "overcome" the light (1:5). Life and light, which are paralleled with each other in the Prologue so that enlightenment and enlivenment are effectively inseparable, come through Christ alone (1:4, 9) and a special emphasis is made that John the Baptist is "not the light" (1:8) but a testifier, a pointer towards the light. Further to this, the *Logos* is the "only son, full of grace and truth" (1:14) and the importance of this in respect of a unique capacity to see God is reinforced soon afterwards (1:18). Moreover, Christ alone gives "power to become children of God" through belief "in his name" (1:12), and the will by which this happens is God's alone (1:13).

The Horizon of Faith

There is then the question of ranking. Christ comes after John the Baptist but *also* comes before him (1:15, 30) and the Greek wordplay in the "who are you?" questions posed to John the Baptist has already been noted (1:19–21). The process of handing over to the greater authority of Christ begins immediately afterwards, first in the question of baptism—by water or by the Holy Spirit—then in two of the disciples of John going off to follow Jesus (1:32–33, 37). The fact that John's baptism is only with water is noted three times (1:26, 31, 33) and we might note that the Spirit is also mentioned three times (1:32–33). The unworthiness of John in respect of Jesus is also something he himself confesses (1:27) and again we should remind ourselves of his later exclamation, "He must increase, but I must decrease" (3:30). Even as the one witnessing and testifying to Jesus, however, there is perhaps a deliberate contrast between John the Baptist being "sent from God" (1:6, 33) and the priests and Levites who questioned him being sent by mere mortals (1:19, 22, 24).

We should note the very early mention in John of the Son of God (1:18, 34, 49) and Lamb of God (1:29, 36). There is no gradual build-up here, but the divinity is stated repeatedly from the outset and, as already mentioned, lots of different titles are already made explicit in the opening chapter. Note also that, in relation to John the Baptist's two mentions of the Lamb of God, there is a progression from Jesus "coming towards him" to watching Jesus "walk by" and therefore go on ahead of him. Two of his disciples then follow Jesus, who, being ahead of them, turns back and asks the opening question regarding what they are seeking.

John's Jesus carries all the authority and the primary initiative, as shared with and given by the Father, with a knowledge and insight that is totally independent of others, except for the Father of course. John's Jesus does not delay using this authority and insight. He immediately tells Simon upon meeting him whose son he is and that he is henceforth to be called Cephas, translated as Peter, the Rock (1:42). He sees Nathanael coming towards him and declares, possibly with a hint of irony or even mild sarcasm, "Here is truly an Israelite in whom there is no deceit!" (1:47). Perhaps by this he means that Nathanael says exactly what he thinks in this instance, given that he has just asked whether anything good can come out of Nazareth. Jesus then declares that he had *already* seen Nathanel under the fig tree before Philip called him, once again highlighting that the principal calling authority is Jesus (1:48).

Next, near the start of the second chapter, we hear Jesus's mother telling the servants at the wedding, "Do whatever he tells you" (2:5) and it is on Jesus's instruction that the six stone water-jars are filled to the brim and some water is drawn out and taken to the chief steward. We should note that it is *in conjunction with this act of drawing*, and most importantly, of course, according to the *presence and behest of Christ* in their midst, that the transformation in question has taken place (2:7–9). Indeed, more will be said later about the imagery of drawing in John, and especially drawing in or towards. A little later on we hear that Christ alone will raise up the true temple, and it is noteworthy that this is a very early explicit mention of the new temple, Christ's body, that would be raised up in three days (2:18–21), rather than only hearing about this claim in second-hand reports of accusations thrown at Jesus at his trial (cf. Matt 26:61; Mark 14:58). This is followed soon afterwards by an explicit note that Jesus "knew all people and needed no one to testify about anyone; for he himself knew what was in everyone" (2:24–25).

At the start of chapter 3 Nicodemus then tells Jesus explicitly that "no one can do these signs that you do apart from the presence of God" (3:2), but in chapter 4 we encounter what, at first, seems a notable deviation from the theme in question, when Jesus asks the Samaritan woman at the well to *give him* a drink, suggesting a need on his part. She finds this request equally confusing and unexpected—a male Jew asking a female Samaritan for a drink in the culture of the time. Jesus then responds to her confusion by telling her that if she "knew the gift of God," and who Jesus was, then she would be *asking him* for a drink (4:7–10). This is subtly developed later in the gospel when, in arresting parallel to the request to give him a drink, we hear Jesus's penultimate words on the cross, "I am thirsty" (19:28), and soon afterwards his side is pierced with a spear and out comes blood and *water* (19:34). In some liturgical traditions this water is paralleled with the water in the story in Exodus 17:1–7 in which Moses strikes the rock in the wilderness at the Lord's command in order to provide water for the people. Note that just after this landmark reference to thirsting we also hear Jesus declare, "It is finished" (19:30). This parallels, as mentioned previously, Jesus describing his "food" as being to do the Father's will and to bring his work to completion (4:34). Again, therefore, water and food imagery resurface side by side at the climax of Christ's passion. While on the subject of chapter 4, it should also be noted that while, at first, the Samaritans' belief in Jesus is through the Samaritan woman's testimony, it is subsequently through Jesus staying and speaking with them directly that they "know that this is truly the Saviour of the world," providing yet another title for Jesus and emphasizing his self-sufficiency in establishing a relation with them (4:42).

At the start of chapter 5 we hear that Jesus simply "knew" that the paralyzed man by the pool had been lying there for a considerable time (5:6) and, after he has healed him, *he* finds the man in the temple, not vice versa—a fittingly symbolic statement (5:14). Later on in the gospel we are assured that he knows what it is that draws people to seek him (6:26) and who will believe, or not believe, and who will betray him (6:64–71; 13:11, 18). Moreover, Jesus is the *one* shepherd of *one* overall flock and no one takes his life from him but he lays it down voluntarily in accordance with the will of the Father (10:16, 18). He alone understands the nature of what is to come and so, as the passion narrative approaches, we hear the high priest, Caiaphas, telling the council of chief priests and Pharisees, "You know nothing at all! You do not understand that it is better for you to have one man die for the people than to have the whole nation destroyed," with an added note that he says this not on his own insight but only in the prophetic capacity of high priest (11:49–51). Ironically, it is this sudden burst of insight among ignorance that effectively seals the plan to put Jesus to death and he therefore heads to a region near the wilderness as the Passover approaches, emphasizing the sense of isolation that his

John's High Christology

uniqueness now causes (11:53–55). A little later on we then also hear the Pharisees saying to one another in exasperation, "You see, you can do nothing. Look, the world has gone after him!" (12:19).

John's version of the passion narrative is very telling in terms of an emphasis on Jesus's uniqueness and aloneness with respect to others, and this begins very subtly with Jesus himself finding the young donkey to sit on for his entry into Jerusalem, with no explicit suggestion of involving the disciples (12:14). This is in a certain contrast to the other gospels (cf. Matt 21:1–3; Mark 11:1–3; Luke 19:29–31—though Mark and Luke do add the fact that the colt in question had "never been ridden," which in itself indicates the unique place of Jesus and yet is absent in John). Moreover, just after Jesus says, "Father, glorify your name" it is for everyone *else's* sake that the voice is heard from heaven saying, "I have glorified it, and I will glorify it again" (12:28–30). It is not for Jesus's benefit and he alone knows this through and through, and it is accompanied by yet another difference of opinion among the onlookers as to what is going on (12:29, and with other instances of differences of opinion occurring in 7:12, 40–43; 9:9, 16; 10:19–21; 11:36–37). Furthermore, Jesus alone "knew that his hour had come" (13:1) and "that the Father had given all things into his hands, and that he had come from God and was going to God" (13:3). He also declares, "No one comes to the Father except through me" (14:6). Christ's self-sufficient knowledge and power is strongly upheld as the great crescendo of his transformative uniqueness in the passion narrative draws ever closer.

A little later in chapter 14 Jesus then says that if one asks something in *his* name, *he* will do it (14:14). One interesting implication of this might be that Christ's doing lies as much in the asking, or in the *being moved to ask*, as it does in the answering. In other words, he alone would be both the authority and the driving activity concerning what was *truly* asked in his name, rather than it simply being on possibly selfish human whim. This way of looking at the matter is supported to a large extent by a repeat of the same idea just after Jesus has described himself as the vine and the disciples as the branches, which includes the condition of abiding in him along with the words "because apart from me you can do nothing" (15:5–7). There is then a third mention of the same idea, in which Christ is the one who chooses the disciples, rather than vice versa, and who appoints them "to go and bear fruit, fruit that will last." At this point, however, Jesus points to the Father as the one who does the giving of whatever is asked for in the Son's name (15:16). The Father is thus the source of *all that will last*, which is important in respect of the developing trinitarian witness on which more will be said below. There is then yet another mention of the exhortation to "ask" in chapter 16, in which it is said that there will be a time when "no one will take your joy from you. On that day you will ask nothing of me" (16:22–23a). This is followed immediately by a repeat of the assurance that "if you ask anything of the Father in my name, he will give it to you," along with the exhortation, "Ask and you will receive, so that your joy may be complete" (16:23b–24). The strong implication is that there is something genuinely *completable* about this asking, and that the completion is achieved by the Father, in and through the Son.

We then hear that it will be on the day that Christ tells the disciples "plainly" about the Father, rather than in "figures of speech," that they will ask in Christ's name, whereas previously they had not done so (16:24–26). This certainly suggests that the *proper capacity for true asking* is inseparable from a trinitarian relation, and the disciples need to appreciate something of this truth. The relation, the indwelling, once established in the disciples' midst, allows for a participation in the trinitarian life that enables both the proper asking and the answering, and furthermore draws things to the point of completion and fullness of joy, at which point no explicit asking will any longer be necessary.

We might note that the disciples immediately seem overly eager to reach the point where they believe Jesus speaks to them plainly. Indeed, they instantly claim that he has just done so, in contrast to the usual Johannine idiom by which *Jesus alone* declares when something of deep significance has truly occurred, not others. He therefore questions whether their belief and their understanding are actually as sure as they suppose, assuring them instead that they "will be scattered, each one to his home," and will leave him *alone* (16:29–32). This is a good point to quote one of the best phrases I have ever heard in a sermon, in the beautiful description offered by Rowan Williams of "the solitude of Our Lord and God, by some great divine comic dénouement, made into the means of our communion."[1] I will let those powerful words speak for themselves, especially in the context of the finding of a shared home through communion in the body and blood of Christ. These are words that, certainly to my mind, find deep resonance in the tone and the development of John.

We also hear that Jesus knows what people want to ask him (16:19 for instance), just as he knows everything that will happen to him (18:4), and, as the thickness of the passion narrative develops, he states that no one on earth has any real power over him (19:11, something already pre-empted in 14:30). Furthermore, he carries his own cross (19:17)—no mention of Simon of Cyrene in John—and the two crucified alongside him are there by way of emphasizing his centrality, Jesus being crucified "between them" (19:18). The added fact that his legs, unlike those of the other two, were not broken, in fulfilment of the scripture (19:32–33, 36–37), should also be noted. Finally, after Jesus rises from the dead, it is on his authority specifically that the net is let down to the right side of the boat when the timing is right for a catch (21:6).

John's high portrayal of Jesus is very crisp and distinctive, according to which he occupies an utterly unique place, and yet there is equally a great emphasis on the one central respect in which Jesus is *not* alone. He is inseparable from the Father. We hear three key mentions of Jesus not being alone in this respect: that "the Son can do nothing on his own, but only what he sees the Father doing" (5:19, with a similar suggestion repeated in 5:30); that "the one who sent me is with me; he has not left me alone, for I always do what is pleasing to him" (8:29); and that, despite the disciples being scattered and leaving him alone, "I am not alone because the Father is with me" (16:32). This is also mirrored in the *absence* of any suggestion in John that Christ is ever forsaken, even on the

---

1. Williams, *Open to Judgement*, 149.

cross, in contrast to the other gospels (cf. Matt 27:46; Mark 15:34, while noting that Luke 23:46 takes a still different approach). In John, the Son's complete union with the Father is eternal and beyond question.

A DEVELOPING SENSE OF THE TRINITY

Right from the outset we have heard implicitly about the relation of the *Logos*, the Word, the Son to the Father (1:1). He is with God and he is God, and it should be noted that the Greek for "with God," *pros ton theon*, takes, grammatically speaking, an accusative case suggestive of an active directedness *towards* God, the Father. One of the earliest explicit statements that develops the nature of the relationship between the Father and the Son, a major theme throughout the gospel, is then encountered quite early on in the declaration, "The Father loves the Son and has placed all things in his hands" (3:35). This is in itself a powerful statement of conveyed authority and is further built upon by mention of the idea that Christ has food to eat that the disciples do not know about, which he then reveals to consist in doing the will of the one who sent him and in completing his work, as already noted (4:31–34).

The next big development of the Father-Son relationship is made explicit when the Jewish authorities first begin persecuting Jesus for healing on the sabbath and he annoys them all the more by calling God his own Father and stating, "My Father is still working, and I also am working" (5:17–18). Placed in its wider context, not least in parallel with the creation account of Genesis 1, this is part of a deep demonstration that the true seventh day fulfilment—in one sense a completion of creation and in another sense its renewal—is effected specifically in Christ, through whom all things were made, and moreover in his passion, death and resurrection, pre-empting once again those immortal words of completion that constitute Jesus's very final utterance on the cross. Noting again the obvious parallel between the Prologue and the opening creation story in Genesis, this thoroughly fulfils the concept of God's finishing and resting (Gen 2:2), not least in the opening of a true resting place for God and humanity *together*—a new Eden. As the light, Christ is then also the deepest fulfilment of the first day light in Genesis 1:3.

Returning to John, from 5:19 until the end of chapter 5 the theme of Jesus's relation to the Father is developed in its first wave of details. The first emphatic point is that the Son does nothing on his own but only what the Father is also doing, and that the Father shows the Son *everything* he is doing (5:19 again). Jesus then further assures people that the Father "will show him greater works than these" (5:20), which is immediately projected onto the theme of resurrection and the giving of life, and indeed new life (5:21). Immediately after this the direction of relation—from Father to Son to those drawn to receive—is reversed and, beginning from the perspective of people, a failure to honour the Son is a failure to honour the Father (5:23, re-echoed in 5:38 in specific reference to those who had started to persecute Jesus). This comes with a further statement to the effect that "all judgement" is given to the Son (5:22) and we should remember that it has already been declared that "God did not send the Son into the world to condemn the world, but in order that the world might be saved through him" (3:17). Judgement and condemnation are in this case two rather different concepts, and judgement can very much be *creative*. Somewhat confusingly on first hearing, it is suggested later on in the gospel that the Father is the judge (8:50), so we have the reciprocal idea that the judge hands judgement over to another who in turn hands back to him as the source of his own sending, testifying, and life-giving authority. The necessary but sufficient condition for mortals specifically is then declared to be hearing the word spoken—or perhaps the Word itself—and believing the one who sent the Word (5:24).

It is then emphasized that because the Father has "life in himself" so too is the Son granted the same, with a repeat mention of the "authority to *execute* judgement," now explicitly stated as being "because he is the Son of Man" (my italics, 5:26–27). The Son of Man reference is one that I will develop in chapter 5, but to set the scene here, and also to guide the unfolding discussion of John's developing trinitarian witness, I think it appropriate to appeal at this point to a guiding analogy concerning the Trinity. The analogy comes from a combination of two theological writers, Hans Urs von Balthasar and Dorothy L. Sayers, both of whom suggest that an analogy concerning the life of the Trinity can be encountered by considering the foundational dynamic of a stage drama, a creative work of art.

Balthasar talks about the "Author," the "Actor," and the "Director,"[2] while Sayers focuses more on the nature of the "Creative Idea" involved in the authorship, the "Creative Energy" or "Activity" according to which the Idea is expressed, and the "Creative Power" by which the meaning of the art in question is impressed both upon the Author and upon the receptive and responsive audience.[3] The concept of the Son—both the Son of God *and* the Son of Man—as the Principal Actor around whose role the dynamic of the drama is creatively organized seems to me to be very fitting to the unfolding of John. Equally appropriate is to consider the role of the Son in terms of the Creative Energy/Activity through whom the Creative Idea of the Father is expressed, as per Sayers. The role of Director, empowering the reception of meaning by all who are drawn to behold and participate in the drama, will be considered further in what follows.

Where the above reference to the *executing* of judgement is concerned, this is expressed within the creation itself according to the *Logos becoming flesh*, journeying through creation in material form in space and time, hence the appropriateness of reference at this point to the Son of Man. At the same time, however, it is still acknowledged that the Creative Activity, as expressed overall through the *Logos*, the Son of God, is not *exhaustively* summarized by reference to this specific "lensing" of experience from a creaturely perspective within creation, as we know it now. This, in turn, feeds into the sense of that which is yet "greater," which will be explored further in the final chapter of this book. Having introduced the analogy, let us now return to the text of John.

2. Balthasar, *Theo-Drama*, 268–305.
3. Sayers, *The Mind of the Maker*, 35–45.

A little further on in chapter 5 the idea of what *constitutes* being "just" in judgement is expressed theologically as the will of the Son not operating in isolation from that of the Father, who sent him for a particular purpose (5:30). This can be related back to the famous, anthem-inspiring declaration, "For God so loved the world that he gave his only Son, so that everyone who believes in him may not perish but may have eternal life" (3:16). Finally, for this section of the gospel, what has already been said about love, life, and judgement in relation to the inseparable bond between the Father and the Son who does the Father's work is repeated regarding *testimony* to the work in question (5:31–37). This is subsequently repeated again later on (8:13–18) where it is also emphasized that the Son does not judge merely "according to the flesh" (appealing here to the Greek text once again).

The next major comment on the Father-Son relation occurs during the bread of life discourse in chapter 6, where it is declared, "Everything that the Father gives me will come to me, and anyone who comes to me I will never drive away" (6:37). This is again because the Son comes to do the will of the Father, which Jesus expresses as meaning "that I should lose nothing of all that he has given me, but raise it up on the last day" (6:38-40), which is a classic text for occasions like All Souls' Day and Remembrance Sunday. Moreover, that which comes to Jesus does so, according to the testimony we find in John, because it is "drawn by the Father" (6:44). It is worth noting here that the Greek word for "drawn" is the same word later used when Jesus declares, "And I, when I am lifted up from the earth [compare this with 3:14], will draw all things/people [there is a textual variant here] to myself" (12:32). Not only that, but the same verb is employed yet again at the end of the gospel, when the disciples encounter the resurrected Christ and he tells them to cast their net to the right side of the boat, whereupon they have so many fish in the net that they cannot "haul" it back in (21:6). This is repeated again a few verses later, when Simon Peter is instructed by Jesus to bring some of the catch and, suddenly, he *is* now able, apparently even on his own, to "haul" the net ashore (21:11). We might notice a progression here: first it is the Father who draws, then this activity is passed to the Son, and then to the disciples. The dynamic and living architecture[4] of the Creative Idea is expressed and communicated through the Son and is then manifested in the texture of creaturely experience and response.

For all that has been said so far it is no surprise of course to find Jesus responding to the question of how he has "such learning" without officially having been instructed (7:15) by again explaining that his teaching is from the one who sent him (7:16) and that those who discern through resolving "to do the will of God" will recognize such teaching (7:17). There is a consistently shared dynamic of sending, judging, and testifying, built up in a manner emphasizing the unity of Father and Son, but with a subtlety of distinction between Christ as Son of God, not *of* this world, and Christ as having become flesh and able to judge *in* the world. At no point, however, is the Son left alone in this sense (8:28–29), even to the apparent earthly end on the cross, and we hear later in chapter 8 that, while the Son seeks the will of the Father and completes his work to the end, the Father is the one who seeks the Son's glory (8:50). The Author of the drama is seeking the perfect performance of the Principal Actor, something of the "zeal" of which has already been communicated earlier in John (2:17), where the disciples "remembered that it was written, 'Zeal for your house will consume me.'" The reference in this case is to Psalm 69:9.

From chapter 9 matters then turn to the incorporation of others into the work of the Son, the one who was *sent*. With the landmark moment of the opening of the eyes of the man born blind, notably something never heard of before (9:32), a radically new way of seeing is strongly pointed towards, a new appreciation of the nature of God through an opening of the relation between Father and Son in the Spirit. Very fittingly therefore, the name of the pool in which the blind man is asked to go and wash is Siloam, meaning "Sent" (9:7). There is an implication of a *sharing* in this sent-ness that also importantly involves an act of washing, and it is probably doubly meaningful for being also "a sabbath day" when

---

4. I pick this word deliberately by reference to its etymology, coming from the Greek for the output of a principal craftsman.

this act of eye opening occurs (9:14). In fact, it is an act that even causes division among the Pharisees themselves as to how they should respond to Jesus (9:16, with a similar division repeated in 10:19-21 when Jesus mentions the laying down of his life and his taking it up again).

The theme of sharing and incorporation is subsequently unfolded and further emphasized in later chapters of the gospel. Chapter 10 brings in the image of the shepherd, who is the Son, and the gatekeeper, by logical implication the Father, who "opens the gate for him" (10:3) and the Son is subsequently identified as both the gate and the good shepherd (10:7-11, 14). It is stated that the reason that the sheep know the shepherd and the shepherd knows the sheep is *rooted* in the fact that the Father knows the Son and the Son knows the Father (10:14-15). Furthermore, it is on the Father's command that the Son has power to lay down his life "in order to take it up again" (10:17-18). There is also a direct identification made between the "hand" of the Son and that of the Father, a hand keeping the sheep eternally safe so that they won't be snatched away, since "the Father and I are one" (10:28-30). At this point stones are once again picked up in anger (10:31) and Jesus responds first by appealing to the Father's "good works" and then defending the blasphemy charge by pointing out that, in the tradition of those accusing him, the coming of the Word of God to someone gave them some exalted status, with a resonance of divine image or likeness being attached to it (10:34-36). When they attempt to arrest him for saying this, in a moment of beautiful Johannine irony, he escapes "from *their hands*" (my italics, 10:39).

It is also at this point in John that Christ explicitly uses the preposition "in" to describe the mutual relation of Father and Son—each being in the other (10:38)—something that will later be developed significantly in chapters 16 and 17, more on which below. Therefore, whoever believes in the Son believes in the Father (12:44) and to see the Son is also to see the Father (12:45; 14:8-9). This logic is further extended to the Son of Man, since, "If God has been glorified in him, God will also glorify him in himself and will glorify him at once" (13:32). When Philip objects that they need to see the Father directly in order to be satisfied (14:8), Jesus repeats the assertion that he is in the Father and the Father is in him (14:10) and adds to this that everything concerning what and how he communicates is part of the works of the Father in him. Philip should at the very *least* believe because of the works, but preferably *also* in the idea of mutual indwelling of Father and Son (14:11). The relation between the Idea and the Activity expressing the Idea, including *back to its own Author*, is made all the clearer in this emphasis on mutual indwelling.

Once the idea of indwelling, including the indwelling Idea, has been introduced and established, we hear then the first explicit mention of the Holy Spirit as Advocate, or *Paraclete* as transliterated from the Greek—the one who calls or invokes alongside someone. This is introduced in conjunction with the declaration, "If you love me, you will keep my commandments. And I will ask the Father, and he will give you another Advocate, to be with you for ever" (14:15–16). This condition is then also given as the reason that this Advocate, the "Spirit of truth," cannot be received by "the world," but the disciples are assured, "You know him, because he abides with you, and he will be in you" (14:17). Once again, this emphasizes a dwelling in and among people, but in a manner that is somewhat *beyond* "the world." Christ's life is then intimately bound up with that of the disciples, and so he declares, "In a little while the world will no longer see me, but you will see me; because I live, you also will live" (14:19). *Knowing* that Father and Son mutually indwell will then be the *result* of the disciples sharing in Christ's life (14:20). The further realization of incorporation and indwelling in Christ is, in turn, enabled by "the Advocate, the Holy Spirit, whom the Father will send in my name" and who will, among other things, "teach" and "remind" the disciples regarding what Jesus has said to them (14:26).

The introduction of the role of the Advocate is then immediately followed by a mention of peace—a juxtaposition that will occur again post-resurrection in what is effectively John's account of the receiving of the Holy Spirit (20:19–22). This peace is qualified as being *not a worldly* peace (14:27), again true to the distancing from the world that we find at various points in John, and which seems similar in tone to the famous description in Philippians 4:7 of "the peace of God, which surpasses all understanding." Rowan Williams, in one of his early works, remarks of this unworldly conception of peace that the difference lies not only in the form of the peace but also in the form of the giving. The Christ of the gospels does not produce immediately and obviously visible harmony, and indeed Williams notes the words of Christ himself that he brings not peace in worldly terms but rather "a sword" (Matt 10:34) and that he wishes that the fire which he came to bring to the earth "were already kindled!" (Luke 12:49).[5] Not only that, but he also has to carry within himself the painful knowledge that the course of action he will need to take will destroy any earthly sense of peace connected with Jerusalem (Luke 19:41–44), one of whose names is "City of Peace." He must accept that his presence is what it is and will do what it will do,[6] being "a sign that will be opposed so that the inner thoughts of many will be revealed" (Luke 2:34–35). This phrase from Luke leaves something of a cliffhanger concerning what this revealing might unveil.

Williams notes not only that "the price of our sitting down in harmony is the echoing discord of the crucifixion" but also that the church could well be viewed as "what is expelled by societies as they struggle with the challenge of God's peace."[7] Christ's presence exposes a tension between the worlds of contentedness and discontentedness, even within one and the same individual, and shows why a simple or trivial "truce" between them will not suffice, as for example in the case of "a fixed pessimism combined with an abstract future hope."[8] Instead, it requires the two worlds to "meet in a perspective wider than the world itself" and furthermore in the one who "refuses to *belong*, but creates a world for others to belong in."[9] That is certainly the tone of John, and with much

---

5. Williams, *The Truce of God*, 65.
6. Williams, *The Truce of God*, 67.
7. Williams, *The Truce of God*, 69.
8. Williams, *The Truce of God*, 72.
9. Williams, *The Truce of God*, 77–78. Italics from Williams.

The Horizon of Faith

complementary material among the other gospels, especially in Luke. Tension can indeed be creative if things are held together in the proper manner, and especially in accordance with the one who alone can effect the necessary containment.

Given the need to move *beyond* the world into a perspective that it simply cannot contain, noting again the tone of the verse on which the gospel overall finishes, suggesting that the world would not contain the books that would need to be written (21:25), Christ prepares the disciples for his "going away." This going away will create the possibility of a *new* means of "coming" to them, and Christ prepares things by saying that they should be glad that he is "going to the Father, because the Father is greater than I" (14:28). This latter comment is of course a very big one when it comes to trinitarian doctrine and I will say more on this particular aspect in the final chapter on the Johannine theme of "greater things." For now, however, it is worth noting how Sayers relates her analogy of Idea, Energy/Activity and Power to this statement. She describes the material incarnation of the expressive Energy or Activity—the physical revealing of the artwork—in parallel to the description of the Son in the Athanasian Creed as "equal to the Father as touching His Godhead and inferior to the Father as touching His manhood." She suggests that the Creative Energy/Activity—her analogy of the *Logos* in this case—should be viewed in similar terms: "Equal to the Idea as touching its essence and inferior to the Idea as touching its expression."[10] Here the expression is precisely that made in material terms, within space and time. That which remains always somewhat beyond the world is the "timeless Idea," which Sayers analogizes with the personality of the author in question.

It is still through the revealed work of the author, however, and especially in that aspect which is expressed in terms of an autobiography, that one can get a better insight as to how the intention of the work or works overall should best be received and interpreted.[11] That having been said, the question of the *degree* to which a materially-expressed work can be formed such as to

---

10. Sayers, *The Mind of the Maker*, 90.
11. Sayers, *The Mind of the Maker*, 89.

John's High Christology

contain such self-expression remains lingering in the background. Indeed, the very consideration of this question affords a greater dimension to the idea of a *tension* between worlds of content-ment and dis-content-ment. In this respect Sayers refers to "the necessary limitations of literary form" as a key aspect of her analogy, as well as emphasizing that the truth of the content of an author's self-revealing will be "tested by the truth of the form" by which it is expressed.[12] It is ultimately through a full awareness and appreciation of such a form that the content and the joy—the content-ment—will be made complete, in this case beyond earthly measure, and we may refer back to John at this point (3:34; 15:11; 16:24; 17:13).

The next addition to the language used to describe the Father-Son relation comes with the comparison between Jesus and the vine, in which he says, "I am the true vine, and my Father is the vine-grower" (15:1). It is also the Father who prunes (15:2) to ensure appropriate overall quantity and quality of harvest. The vine metaphor builds on the idea of mutual abiding (15:4–5) in an intimate connection between vine and branches. This section of John sees increasingly frequent mention of the word "love." The repeated exhortation to "abide in my love" (15:9–10) precedes a repeat mention of the commandment "that you love one another as I have loved you" (15:12, previously stated in 13:34). The centrality of love is inseparable from the manner in which John's account of the nature of God is built up, centered on the three distinctive Persons of Father, Son, and Holy Spirit that this involves. The disciples get granted a progressively increased and articulated share in this, alongside mention of the Advocate, whom Christ will send from the Father—an assurance mentioned three times (14:16; 14:26; 15:26)—and with whom the disciples "also are to testify" (15:27). Moreover, to ensure that this Advocate is not falsely viewed as somehow separate from the relation between the other two Persons of the Trinity, it is stated explicitly that the Spirit of truth does "not speak on his own, but will speak whatever he hears," and furthermore that he is involved in the glorification of the Son.

---

12. Sayers, *The Mind of the Maker*, 90–91.

He takes what is both the Father's and the Son's and declares it (16:13–15).

Chapter 17 then draws the build-up of what we would now think of as a trinitarian faith to a great crescendo that emphasizes the key theme of mutual indwelling. It begins with the exhortation to the Father, "Father, the hour has come; glorify your Son so that the Son may glorify you, since you have given him authority over all people, to give eternal life to all whom you have given him" (17:1–2). Eternal life is then expressed as being *in itself* fully to know the Father and the Son whom he sent (17:3). In terms of the stage drama analogy from Balthasar and Sayers, we could think of this as the *fullest possible awareness* of the artwork that creaturely form and relation can collectively accommodate, within the context of the entire created arena—the *open stage*. The openness is here as much an openness to transformation as anything else. In terms of the language used by Sayers, the Creative Idea of the Author is inseparably related to the manner and form according to which it is expressed by the Creative Activity, the center of gravity of which, in Balthasar's terms, has its locus in the Principal Actor. This locus *draws in* other participant actors, with accompanying meaning and power, in accordance with the role of the Director, the Advocate in this case. The "stage" in this sense strongly *relates* to the world but is not entirely contained by it.

There is a distinctively eternal tone in this address to the Father in chapter 17, given especially that Jesus declares, "I glorified you on earth by finishing the work that you gave me to do" (17:4), which to our normal sense of chronology might seem strange, since the declaration of completion itself does not occur until chapter 19 and yet the *past* tense is already used in chapter 17. Maybe the key moment is deemed to have occurred in Jesus's previous, obedient acceptance (12:27–28; 13:31–32), but this is not clear. The tone with which the glory is spoken about at the start of chapter 17 is one that actively involves the *result* of what is happening in the midst of those mortal creatures over which the Son has been given authority. A few verses later we hear a distinctive but nonetheless complementary tone, when Jesus says, "Father, glorify me in your own presence with the glory that I had in your presence before the world existed" (17:5). There is a clear two-fold sense to the glory: the glory that was and is and will always be co-eternal with the Father; and the glory that specifically results from an unfolding *incarnational journey* through the creation that came through the Son in the first place.

If we compare this briefly with the famous story of the prodigal son in Luke 15:11–32, then we find two examples of sonhood: the one who remains with his father in his true homeland; and the one who takes what his father gives him and travels to a far-off land. Clearly, in the parable in question, both sons are significantly flawed, since the elder son is resentful and the younger son profligate and wasteful. Yet, very fittingly, the one telling the parable is the perfect and simultaneous example of what both aspects of sonhood *could be*. He is both the perfectly obedient Son who is co-eternal with the Father, in that initial and ultimate homeland concerning which the question of where-ness is so frequently directed in John, and also the Son who journeys into a different form of dwelling-place in becoming flesh and, far from wasting what is given to him, instead *loses nothing* of it, as John has already given Jesus as declaring (6:39).

Indeed, so foundational is the Father-Son relation in John that it is said that the very essence of eternal life is in itself knowing that relation—knowing it *as an incorporated participant* in that which results from the Son completing the Father's work and drawing creation to himself in order to establish a new creation in himself (12:32 and 17:3–4 combined). Furthermore, it involves knowing Father and Son as distinct and yet as inseparable, in the power of the Holy Spirit, as the church has received and expressed the matter in her traditional teaching. In John 17 the mutual indwelling involved becomes especially strongly emphasized, with repeated mention of the point: "As you, Father, are in me and I am in you, may they also be in us" (17:21); "that they may be one, as we are one, I in them and you in me, that they may become *completely* one" (my italics, 17:22–3); and "so that the love with which you have loved me may be in them, and I in them" (17:26).

This is notably paralleled with a development in relation to the world: first the world is to "believe" that the Father has sent the Son (17:21); then it is to "know" this, and also that the Father has loved those in the Son even as he loves the Son himself (17:23); and then those given to the Son are to be with the Son where he truly is in order to see his glory fully—to see that which was given to the Son because the Father loved the Son "before the foundation of the world" (17:24). The foundation for subsequent trinitarian doctrine is well and truly laid here.

THE PASSION AND POST-RESURRECTION NARRATIVES ACCORDING TO JOHN'S CHRISTOLOGY

From the start of chapter 18 onwards the thick of the passion narrative moves forward. John's high Christology is demonstrated in several places within both the passion and the resurrection narratives. On hearing the words "I am [he]" those having come to arrest Jesus fall to the ground (18:6). John locates the trial and crucifixion on "the day of Preparation for the Passover" itself, thereby emphasizing the identification between Jesus and the sacrificial Lamb of God (19:14, cf. 13:1). We might also well reflect on the irony of those accusing Jesus taking him to Pilate, on whom they were effectively relying to do the dirty work of pronouncing a death sentence on their behalf, and yet not entering Pilate's residence in order "to avoid ritual defilement and to be able to eat the Passover," while the true Passover Lamb is about to be revealed in a manner they have not foreseen (18:28-31; 19:6-7). The identification with the day of Preparation also makes the coinciding of the sabbath—"a day of great solemnity"—with the period between Christ's death and resurrection (19:31) both potent and ironic, with the true sabbath rest being profoundly initiated in Christ's final words, "It is finished" (19:30 again), and the profoundest of all new weeks being opened up beyond, first encountered "while it was still dark" (20:1).

John's High Christology

Overall, John also makes a somewhat larger emphasis on Jesus as a king, and especially on the tension surrounding the claim to sovereignty, than in the other gospels (18:33, 36-37; 19:2-3, 5, 14-15, 19-22). As already noted, the mention of those crucified alongside him in John emphasizes only that Jesus is at the *center* (19:18) and there is no suggestion of any dialogue between them and Christ. Instead, we hear words directed towards "his mother and the disciple whom he loved," encouraging the beginning of a new family of discipleship (19:26-7). We ought also to note the mention of Christ's "seamless" tunic, "woven in one piece *from the top*" (my italics, 19:23). We might hear an echo here of the other gospel accounts that parallel Jesus's death with the tearing open of the temple curtain "from top to bottom" (Matt 27:51; Mark 15:38, cf. Luke 23:45, though Luke does not specify that it was from top to bottom) and such top-down emphasis is clearly suggestive of divine initiative and purpose. By, in a sense, transferring the "from the top" imagery to Jesus's *own vestiture* the association with his body and the temple is arguably strengthened. Equally, the fact that it is *not* in this case torn, in addition to the actions of the soldiers being in fulfilment of the scripture (19:24), could also be taken in a Christological light—Christ's humanity in seamless union with his divinity in the context of an implicit aspect of temple imagery surrounding his body, and again befitting John's high Christology. Any symbolism here is admittedly somewhat ambiguous, but the absence of tearing does resonate somewhat with the fact that, in John, we find no hint of any mention that Christ had been forsaken by the Father on the cross.

Finally, where the passion narrative is concerned, there is also the emphasis on the "new tomb in which no one had ever been laid" (19:41), once again emphasizing Jesus's place as distinctive from that of others. This is further developed in the narrative of the empty tomb after the resurrection of Jesus, referencing "the cloth that had been on Jesus' head, not lying with the linen wrappings but rolled up in a place by itself" (20:7). In conjunction once again with the ever-lingering question of where-ness in John, there is clearly something distinctive in John about the head of Jesus, the Anointed One, whom only God can anoint "from the top" as it were, while humanity instead anoints his feet (12:3 again, and noting that this is in the context of looking ahead to Jesus's burial in the tomb, as he himself indicates in 12:7). Similarly, the angels who appear in the empty tomb sit where the body had been, distinctively with "one at the head and the other at the feet" (20:12). The divine and human aspects of John's Christology are, like the tunic, woven together into a seamless whole that John gradually explores and unfolds. The greatest mystery is associated with the place of the head of Christ, hence the fittingness of the cloth in question being *rolled up* in this distinctive place—something yet to be fully unfolded in the new life of the resurrection.

In terms of the gospel's post-resurrection Christology, we should also remind ourselves that in John's account the Holy Spirit is given to the disciples directly through Jesus's breath (20:22). There are of course similarities between this and the account of the Day of Pentecost in Acts 2:1–4, since in both cases the disciples are gathered "together in one place," and in both cases there is the classic imagery of the Spirit as wind or breath. We could also add that in both cases an unexpected presence breaks into the house or room in question. In the Acts of the Apostles, the sequel to the Gospel of Luke, there is no explicit mention of the giving of peace at Pentecost, which has instead already been noted in the account of Christ's appearance among the gathering of disciples in Luke 24:36. John's version of the giving of the Holy Spirit seems closer to the intimacy of God's breathing in Genesis 2:7, which also fits with the other links to aspects of Genesis creation imagery that we find in John: the opening words "in the beginning"; subtle references to garden imagery (18:1; 19:41; 20:15); and the question of where humanity's truly intended dwelling-place is to be found. There is, among other things, an intimacy of association implied between the figure of Christ and the Lord God who walks in the garden (Gen 3:8), especially, as already noted, in the telling and penetrating question, "Where are you?" (Gen 3:9).

John's High Christology

APPRECIATING THE PLACE OF OUR PARTICIPATION

To return then to the question of our place, and to the question with which this chapter began —whether we are really part of this—we can see in the development of John's high Christology and trinitarian witness the firm contours of the affirmative "yes." To appeal to the combined analogies of Balthasar and Sayers, the eternal Idea of the Author is expressed according to the Principal Actor around whose organizing Activity a specific form of self-revealing *open* to the audience is brought about. This occurs in inseparable accordance with the Director who guides, reminds, and accompanies in such a manner as to promote and to emphasize the Creative Power of the meaning involved for both Author and audience, and for the drawing of the latter towards the former. This occurs *both* "before the foundation of the world," in the timeless aspect of the Creative Idea, *and* within the bonds of spacetime and matter, in distinctive but complementary manners that find their union in Christ. Furthermore, as Williams says, the stage upon which such self-revealing is made manifest also draws the imagination towards the need for a space for our *belonging* that lies beyond any perspective which is completely containable in this world.

The "yes" given here, however, it not trivial, and it is much more a beginning than it is an end. It *empowers* active, creaturely involvement and, rather than simply dropping on our doorstep, it draws us away from those individual homes to which we would otherwise be scattered and towards the newly prepared dwelling-place in which our lives are filled with the supreme theological relevance of the life of Christ and the life of the Trinity. John in particular shows us that this new life is far *more relevant* than anything that we may seek simply on the basis of day-to-day convenience and instant accessibility now, and it is one requiring commitment of exploration. Our day-to-day sense of existence can, and of course does, throw many distractions in our path, and it is now therefore to the question of tackling such distractions, so as to gain a progressively deeper appreciation of the journey that we are on, that we need to turn in the following chapter.

Chapter 4

Seeing the Wood for the Trees
Not Being Distracted From the Journey

THE WEEK OF ALL WEEKS

During my time at theological college the biggest occasion of the college's year was without doubt Holy Week. For those of us who were studying full-time, participation in the entirety of the week in question was considered obligatory, and this involved a lot of activity and organization. Everything began with Evening Prayer on the Saturday before Palm Sunday, and then for Palm Sunday itself—followed by Holy Monday, Holy Tuesday, and Holy Wednesday—there was Morning Prayer, then the main Liturgy of the Day, then Evening Prayer, and finally Compline each day. Then there was the set of traditional services for Maundy Thursday and Good Friday, along with Morning and Evening Prayer when it did not clash with a main service time, and then, on Holy Saturday, getting everything ready for a massive Easter Vigil beginning at sunrise on Easter morning and lasting the best part of three hours, then Easter breakfast, and then…Easter Matins! In addition to this there were the usual college domestic duties allocated among the students, special Holy Week lectures, obviously also eating together, and, for the three big days of the Triduum itself—Maundy Thursday, Good Friday, and Holy Saturday—looking after guests who were with us for the occasion. It was a week with a massively distinctive feel to it, and very suitably so.

Most people's encounter with Holy Week is understandably and often inevitably conducted so as to fit around their routine and to work with their various other commitments as far as possible. While very understandable, there is also a sense in which this misses out on something. One thing about being utterly *immersed* in the setting of a theological community throughout the whole of the week in question that really stuck out to me, especially in my first year of experiencing it, was quite how much more you come to realize concerning how much the details of Holy Week actually encompass. The week is rather like a microcosm, in the sense that the events and meaning contained within it can speak to such a wide variety of life's questions, hopes, challenges, and circumstances. To be immersed in the thick of the ongoing liturgical activity and accompanying lectures and reflections is to be in a good position to spot some of the deeply rooted connections that the week involves. When you consider that a hefty section of each of the gospels involves the events between Christ's entry into Jerusalem and the account of his resurrection, it is not surprising that the thicket of scriptural links and cross-references alone is really very sizeable. This is before we even start including additional reflections and activities, such as Stations of the Cross and lectures on the liturgical development that occurred around marking Holy Week in the early centuries of the church. If anyone gets the opportunity to go on an immersive Holy Week retreat I would wholeheartedly recommend it. It is a great means of appreciating the depth of what can be encountered in the relative absence of distraction from the prevailing theme.

John places a great emphasis on the importance of a proper means of seeing and attending, always directing attention forwards to the one who goes ahead of us and needs to be followed, even if the finer details of what is involved differ from one individual to another. It is noticeable that *different* aspects of Jesus's life and witness are made explicit in this regard in comparison with the other gospels, and this stands out as much in terms of what is left out as what is included. John seems to keep focus on particular threads, and this book suggests one way in which we might trace those threads with eyes kept open for the subtlety and implication that they weave together.

JOHN'S PRESENCES AND ABSENCES

To begin with, there is no explicit birth narrative in John, who emphasizes instead the supra-cosmic dimension of Christ's origin. I mentioned the work of Sayers in the previous chapter, and, among other things, she considers the degree to which the concept of *autobiography* is appropriate when reflecting on the manner in which the Creative Energy or Activity—the Actor in Balthasar's terms—expresses the Creative Idea, the intention of the Author, in the *uniquely specific* case of the Incarnation. She points out that one especially salient aspect of the analogy is that a human author may freely choose the point in the series of their works at which the autobiographical work appears and, furthermore, that the *reasoning* behind the choice in question may or may not explicitly be given.[1] In John such explicit reference to the manner and place of Christ's birth is a notable absence, with the emphatic presence being instead on the reasoning relating to the *Logos*, the Son of God, revealing himself in the way that he does in accordance with the eternal relation he has with the Father before the creation came into existence (17:24 again). This an idea also echoed in other New Testament writings, of course, such as Ephesians 1:4; Colossians 1:15, 18; 1 Peter 1:20; and Revelation 13:8, to name some of the most explicit, as well as reference to Christ as "the Alpha" in Revelation 1:8. John takes an emphatically bigger-picture view from the outset, as already noted in chapter 1.

The manner and place of the birth itself is by no means the only aspect not made explicit in John. The mere suggestion of the

---

1. Sayers, *The Mind of the Maker*, 89.

baptism of Jesus, in terms of his receiving baptism from another, is cast very differently in John and somewhat by implication. The "Spirit descending" on Jesus (1:32–33), reported by John the Baptist apparently after the event, seems to be associated more with an emphasis on the greater meaning and power of the baptism Christ *brings* rather than that which he might implicitly be being suggested to have received. This is further developed in the narrative between Jesus and Nicodemus with the importance of being born "from above" or alternatively "anew" (3:3) and the need for this to occur by both water and the Spirit in order to effect a transformation that the flesh cannot (3:5–6).

We also find no explicit mention of the beheading of John the Baptist, but very strong implication of John fading out in order for Jesus to come ever more strongly into focus (3:25–30). Moreover, there is no explicit transfiguration narrative, which is especially interesting when one considers that the other gospels mention Jesus taking Peter, James, and *John* with him as witnesses to this event (Matt 17:1; Mark 9:2; Luke 9:28). Maybe it just isn't the same John, or the witness in this case took Christ's exhortation to remain silent about the event (Matt 17:9; Mark 9:9–10; Luke 9:36) with considerable earnestness. We could equally consider, however, that the *meaning* of the transfiguration, especially with respect to the pending breaking in of a new creation and the emphasis on the *greater* that is yet to come—the focus of the next chapter—is something *implicitly* and *continually* unfolded in John, not least owing to his high Christology and his clear emphasis on the particular efficacy of the flesh of the Son of Man as transformative food for eternal life.

We should also note, on this point, that while there is no explicit institution narrative concerning bread and wine as the body and blood of Christ in John, the water and the bread of life are concepts that, overall, receive a more thorough treatment in John as a key connecting thread in the narrative, as mentioned earlier. Furthermore, John gets to the Lamb of God and the new temple imagery early on, and subsequently makes the identification of the bread of life with the flesh of Christ, with an accompanying mention of the blood of the Son of Man, which could scarcely be expressed more strongly and consequently causes significant dispute (6:51–61).

In fact, there is an added subtlety here, in that John does share with the other gospels the account of Jesus feeding the five thousand, with the mention of five loaves and of the twelve baskets being left over. The number symbolism is well known here, with five standing for the Torah, the Law, the five Books of Moses—Genesis to Deuteronomy—and twelve for the nation of Israel and the association with the twelve tribes. The symbolic thrust of the narrative therefore demonstrates a context in which the true meaning and purpose of the Torah is able to nourish a far deeper sense of national identity than may at first be apparent, while simultaneously addressing the still underlying question as to where enough food was to be found for all those present. This question is addressed specifically in the context of the presence of Christ, who "blessed" (Greek, *eulogēsen*) the loaves in Matthew, Mark, and Luke.

In Matthew and Mark this is complemented by an account of the feeding of the four thousand (Matt 15:29–39; Mark 8:1–21), with mention of seven loaves and seven baskets remaining, and in which Jesus distributes to the crowds "after giving thanks" (Greek, *eucharistēsas*) over the loaves. Once again, the numbers are key, with seven standing for completion and four standing for the earth—the four winds, four corners, four points of the compass, four seasons, and so forth. Here the feeding event speaks to a transformation of the previous context, in which the food Christ provides becomes relevant to the *whole earth* and draws it to *completion*, accompanied by the use of a Greek word from which we clearly derive the word eucharist. John may lack this second feeding account as an explicit event, but the gospel as a whole has more to say *overall* than the other gospels about the relation of the *Logos*, the Son of God, to "the world" and, as will be mentioned in the following chapter, is equally implicit in its use of number symbolism, not least where the number seven is concerned—considering the seven signs for a start. This is to say nothing of the already noted theme of bringing the Father's work to completion and the parallel with Genesis in this regard.

Furthermore, John uses the phrase "when he had given thanks" (6:11—*eucharistēsas* again) in his account of the feeding of the five thousand, while in Matthew and Mark this only occurs in the follow-on account of the feeding of the four thousand. It is as if something of the context of the wider opening that is to follow is already incorporated into John's initial account. Interestingly, the feeding of the five thousand, in John's account, ends with the mention that those witnessing the sign "began to say, 'This is indeed the prophet who is to come into the world'" (6:14), which already implicitly looks towards something else to come in relation to the world—John's alternative, if you like, to the opening up of number symbolism in the feeding of the four thousand. Not long afterwards we do indeed find the matter *fleshed out* in the bread of life discourse.

It is also fitting that it is at this point, the point of transition from the previous water-based symbolism to the solid food of the bread-based symbolism, that it is mentioned that Jesus "realized that they were about to come and take him by force to make him king" and so "withdrew again to the mountain by himself" (6:15). The *journey must continue* according to the manner in which he is sent, rather than allow people to halt proceedings prematurely with a self-imposed event of their own desiring, based on their own immediate conclusions or assumptions regarding the one who is coming into the world and his relation to the world. It is the relational form and relevance of the presence of Christ that seems to matter most in John, and the relevance is implicitly pervasive throughout the threading together of the gospel narrative overall. It is structured in its more *holistic* relation to place and, as will be emphasized further in what follows, also to time, while being explicitly developed in particular contexts at various landmark points, involving signs, symbols, and various other subtleties.

The Horizon of Faith

JOHN'S WORLD AND "THE WORLD"

John contains a sizeable peppering of references concerning "the world" in relation to God and to Christ, while also being the gospel that most emphasizes being *in* the world but not *of* the world—among other things, not being unduly distracted by certain aspects of it. There is, at one point, an explicit question posed as to how Jesus will reveal himself to his disciples but *not* simultaneously "to the world" (14:22) and Jesus's relational response is simply, "Those who love me will keep my word, and my Father will love them, and we will come to them and make our home with them" (14:23). With the Father being the sender of the Word, in the Son, the consistent pattern is *from* the Father, *through* and *in* the Son, and then a returning back to the Father. Father and Son simultaneously indwell one another and such indwelling acts, again from the Father through the Son, to draw disciples into this mutual indwelling. The world then provides a somewhat double-edged arena in this regard, as John presents it.

It is instructive to look at a complete list of references to the world in John at this point—taken here as each case where the Greek word *kosmos* is used—in order to get a feel for the dimensions of consideration involved.

First of all, we hear that the Word and true light "was coming into the world," which "came into being through him" and yet "did not know him" (1:9–10). Similar mention of coming "into the world" is later repeated in relation to "judgement" in the face of the light (3:19), "the prophet" (6:14), "the Messiah, the Son of God" (11:27), another mention of "light" (12:46), and with Jesus informing Pilate about the reason that he "came into the world," namely "to testify to the truth" (18:37). Once again, we find several dimensions of relation to the world noted in accordance with John's high Christology.

In the order in which they occur, other references to the world as are follows:

1. John the Baptist proclaims, "Here is the Lamb of God who takes away the sin of the world!" (1:29).

2. The famous assurance that "God so loved the world that he gave his only Son" and "did not send the Son into the world to condemn the world, but in order that the world might be saved through him" (3:16–17, with a similar note repeated in 12:47).

3. The Samaritans declare that "this is truly the Saviour of the world" (4:42).

4. Jesus explains that "the bread of God . . . gives life to the world" (6:33, further reinforced in relation to his flesh in 6:51).

5. Jesus's brothers ask him to show himself "to the world" and Jesus responds by pointing out the difference between his time, which is "not yet come," and their time, which "is always here." He then further declares to them, "The world cannot hate you," while adding that it hates him because of his testimony regarding the evil it does (7:4–7).

6. Christ is "the light of the world" (8:12, repeated in 9:5).

7. Jesus tells the Pharisees that they "are of this world," but that he is not (8:23).

8. Jesus explains, "I came into this world for judgement so that those who do not see may see, and those who do see may become blind" (9:39).

9. Jesus observes, "Those who walk during the day do not stumble, because they see the light of this world" (11:9).

10. The exasperation of the Pharisees, "Look, the world has gone after him!" (12:19)

11. Jesus remarks that "those who hate their life in this world will keep it for eternal life" (12:25).

12. Jesus declares, "Now is the judgement of this world; now the ruler of this world will be driven out" (12:31).

13. "Jesus knew that his hour had come to depart from this world and go to the Father. Having loved his own who were in the world, he loved them to the end" (13:1).

14. Reference to "the Spirit of truth, whom the world cannot receive" (14:17).

15. Jesus declares, "In a little while the world will no longer see me, but you will see me" (14:19).

16. Jesus explains, in relation to the giving of peace, "I do not give to you as the world gives" (14:27).

17. Jesus tells the disciples that "the ruler of this world is coming. He has no power over me; but I do as the Father has commanded me, so that the world may know that I love the Father" (14:30–31).

18. We hear that the world "hated" Christ first, before it persecutes the disciples, and he has chosen the disciples "out of the world" because they "do not belong to the world" and so they will be hated by the world (15:18–19).

19. The Advocate "will prove the world wrong about sin and righteousness and judgement" (16:8). It is noteworthy here that the mention of righteousness is clarified with the words "because I am going to the Father and you will see me no longer" (16:10). Righteousness is to do with having rightness in *relation*, primarily with God, but also, by extension, with others. There is therefore something about Christ's going from the world to the Father that not only shows his own righteousness but opens up a whole new dimension where right relation with God is concerned, and thereby also with others. The mention of judgement is further clarified as being the result of "the ruler of this world" being condemned (16:11), which highlights the error of a ruling or prevailing judgement in the world's eyes and a tension between that and the judgement executed according to the *Logos* who becomes flesh in the world but not in a manner that is of the world.

20. Christ tells the disciples that there will be a "little while" when they "will weep and mourn, but the world will rejoice," which he likens to a woman in labor pains, but the

joy of the child being brought "into the world" overtakes the pain (16:19–21).

21. Jesus declares, "I am leaving the world and am going to the Father" (16:28).

22. Jesus warns the disciples, "In the world you face persecution. But take courage; I have conquered the world!" (16:33)

23. Jesus expresses the glory that the Son had in the Father "before the world existed" (17:5, with a similar note repeated in 17:24).

24. Jesus says to the Father, "I have made your name known to those whom you gave me from the world" (17:6) and then adds, "I am not asking on behalf of the world, but on behalf of those whom you gave me" (17:9).

25. Almost immediately afterwards he adds, "And now I am no longer in the world, but they are in the world" (17:11).

26. And then, "I speak these things in the world so that they may have my joy made complete in themselves" (17:13). This highlights that what is done and said *in* the world, but not *of* it, is directed towards a completion of the Father's work given to the Son within the world, and there is something unique that can be achieved, a new creation in some sense "out of" the world, by this specifically being said and done "in the world." Chapter 17 also emphasizes the tension surrounding the place of the world with regard to completion and contentment, or of being *properly contained*—held together in the proper manner, according to the right form of relation.

27. In the very next verse we hear that "the world has hated them because they do not belong to the world, just as I do not belong to the world" (17:14, with a repeat mention of neither them nor Christ belonging to the world in 17:16).

28. Jesus says to the Father, "I am not asking you to take them out of the world" (17:15).

29. Jesus continues, "As you have sent me into the world, so I have sent them into the world" (17:18).

30. Jesus asks, "As you, Father, are in me and I am in you, may they also be in us [some authorities have "be one in us" at this point], so that the world may believe that you have sent me" (17:21), and also "that they may be completely one, so that the world may know that you have sent me" (17:23). Note again that this section of narrative leads into the *garden setting* at the start of chapter 18, revisiting an original setting of intended *unity of dwelling-place*—God and humanity together—in which tension and a succumbing to deceit require the demonstration of a unity on the far side of that tension. Such a demonstration is about dramatically to unfold in the chapters that follow in John.

31. Jesus declares, "Righteous Father, the world does not know you, but I know you; and these know that you have sent me" (17:25).

32. Jesus answers the high priest's questioning by saying, "I have spoken openly to the world" (18:20).

33. Jesus explains to Pilate, "My kingdom is not from this world" (18:36). After the subsequent remark that "for this I came into the world, to testify to the truth" (18:37) Pilate asks his infamous question, "What is truth?" (18:38) and references to the world now fizzle out as the pivotal demonstration of the passion itself takes center stage.

34. The final verse of all, assuring us that were everything concerning the Activity of the Word, the Son of God and Son of Man, to be written down, "the world itself could not contain the books that would be written" (21:25).

A few observations are in order here. It is pretty obvious, when we look at the list of references back-to-back, that many of the references in the earlier sections relate primarily to the question of light, life, and salvation, with some added comments about the tense relation of judgement with respect to a testimony both *of* the world and *regarding* the world. There is a clear link between sin and darkness or obscurity, and the light is presented as both revealing and exposing. This is complemented by reference to God's love for the world in contrast to the world's hatred of God and of that which is "of God," refusing to *view* it in the manner that God intended it. There is also an early reinforcement of the Word and the light being in the world but not of the world.

The light's entry into the world transforms what it is to see properly. In the capacity of the sacrificial Lamb of God this entry into the world also takes away sin, which, along with an emphasis on God's love for the world, is among the very first of the references to the world in John. Although not explicit in mentioning the world, the post-resurrection account of Christ's appearance by the Sea of Tiberias does refer to the total number of a hundred and fifty-three fish that were caught by the net on Christ's behest (21:11), and one commonly spread speculation on the relevance of this number is that it represents the number of known fish species at the time and therefore thoroughly represents all people across the world. The opening and ending notes are very positive in this respect, but there is much challenge and development in between.

The world, in the Pharisees' eyes, goes after Jesus (12:19) but the situation—and indeed the question of *situatedness*—presented overall by John is far more double-edged. There is instead something *drawn out* of the world, in a sharp distinction between seeing and not seeing that is thereby revealed. Those who "come and see" and who "hate" their life in this world are the beneficiaries of what is being brought in by the light and Word of God. By stark contrast, those who are determined, or self-determined, that they do *already* see, but do not do so in the right way, are the ones caught by the light in an awkward manner.

Where the world's attitude to the disciples is concerned, we will of course notice that there is a progression from the world not being able to hate them, to it hating them because it hated Christ first. Then we hear that he has *chosen* them out of the world, but does not ask them to be *taken* out of the world. This is followed by the assurance that Christ has conquered the world and the declaration to the Father that the world *has hated* them, as if once again from a projected future prospective or summary. Something distinctive is happening with regard to time. What Christ at first refers to as the disciples' time—that which is "always here" (7:6)—leads directly into his remark that the world cannot hate them. Once they begin to be drawn into his time, oriented towards the significance of his "hour," it will become a different matter, however. Then the world's hatred is noticed and, in addition to an assurance of having conquered the world, Christ seems to pose a countering remark that people keep their life for eternal life if they hate their life in this world. This sounds highly confrontational at first. Faith is clearly much *more* than an attitude of present dissatisfaction regarding the world, and these words surely indicate a sense of priority as much as anything else. They pose the question about whether earthly existence is both the initial and ultimate consideration—the implied answer being "no," since there is a greater aspect to life in John. Among other possible implications, it could also be suggested that people should hate the *part* they are capable of playing *in* the world's hatred.

The references to the world notably clump up around chapters 16 and 17 as the conversing reaches a pre-passion crescendo. The sharp distinction between the world and what Christ chooses and draws out of the world has been laid down in chapter 14, in which the world cannot receive the Spirit of truth because it does not recognize Christ's manner of giving, since Christ does not give as the world gives. In a relatively short period of Christ's time, as his hour approaches, we find a considerable transformation expressed in his relating of the disciples to the *Father* rather than to the world. We have already seen the opening of the invitation to follow him in a manner that he had previously told them that they could not, and now the "hour" will issue in a transformation as of the woman in labor pains receiving her child, paralleled with the mention of the disciples' joy in their new abode being made complete. In the net behind the boat in chapter 21 they are then directed to drag a sign of that fruit, and its completeness, ashore to meet with the resurrected Christ. As the final verse of the gospel then emphasizes, this is a form of completeness, and indeed a form of *abode* and even a *way of being*, that the world cannot fundamentally contain in or of itself. An open beyond-ness predominates.

Just for the sake of completion at this point, we should remember that John also has no explicit account of the Ascension of Christ as a witnessed event but implies it strongly in Jesus's words concerning the Son's relation to the Father as developed *throughout* the gospel, being drawn out of this world in a manner that can only achieve what it does because the Son has also come into the world. This is then highlighted more directly in the exhortation to Mary Magdalene, "Do not hold on to me, because I have not yet ascended to the Father" (20:17). As already noted, there is also the distinctive account of the giving of the Holy Spirit, and no explicit mention of Pentecost as an event. John's is very much an account making fullest use of a sense of the holistic, and in many places also the implicit, throughout the development of a more pervasive context concerning the relation of the light and the Word to place and to time. It consistently teases out the underlying meaning of Christ's journey into and through the world according to a dynamic and always forward-moving relation. This involves something highly distinctive and transformative regarding Christ's time and Christ's hour, about which some further reflection is merited.

GOD'S TIME AND CHRIST'S "HOUR"

The first mention of Jesus's hour is found in his words to his mother—"My hour has not yet come" (2:4)—in the context of the pre-emptive transformation at the wedding at Cana. The fuller significance of this becomes apparent subsequently in the gospel, and will be reflected on later. The next mention is to the Samaritan woman at the well—"the hour is coming" (4:21) and, shortly afterwards, "the hour is coming, and is now here" (4:23a)—both in reference to the true worship of the Father *not* being tied to a particular mountain but rather something connected with the "spirit and truth" according to which the Father *seeks* people to worship him (4:23b). We may perhaps notice something of a parallel here between the seeking that is of the Father and that which is asked of the disciples, recalling again Jesus's opening question in 1:38. It is also interesting that, on the first two occasions that the idea of the coming hour is mentioned, Christ is addressing a woman, while it is also a woman—Mary Magdalene—who, in John, first explicitly encounters the new dawn, the new time, of the resurrected Christ (20:1). All three of these women are addressed by Jesus simply as "Woman," which sounds rather rude to modern ears of course. Mary Magdalene is addressed in this manner twice, once by the two angels in white (20:13), who ask why she is weeping, and once by the at first unrecognized Jesus (20:15), who asks both why she is weeping and also whom she is *seeking*—the same Greek word as in 1:38 and 4:23. Finally, he then addresses her *by name* directly in order to move her to a new recognition (20:16), and in this *new time* opened up in the resurrection there remains that further "not yet" reference when he instructs her not to cling to him because his ascension has yet to occur (20:17).

In addition to the sense of "not yet," however, the sense of being *already here* in relation to a coming hour is further echoed by Jesus telling the disciples, "The reaper is already receiving wages and is gathering fruit for eternal life, so that sower and reaper may rejoice together" (4:36). Moreover, the power of Jesus to state and to transform the significance of time, or of a particular hour, is emphasized when the royal official whose son Jesus heals from a distance realizes, upon asking his servants what hour his son began to recover, that it was the hour when Jesus had said to him that his son would live, specifically the seventh hour (4:52–53, with the time reference taken from the Greek text). We should further note here that the previous encounter with the Samaritan woman was around the sixth hour (4:6, from the Greek text again), so the number symbolism has moved forward, as it were.

Later on, we hear that it is also about the sixth hour when Jesus is handed over to be crucified (19:14, Greek text), the event which necessarily comes before the pending completion proclaimed by Jesus's final words on the cross (19:30). This parallel in number symbolism lends extra thrust to the aforementioned repeat of Jesus's expression of thirst (4:7; 19:28). Very fittingly therefore, it is also in between these two mentions of a particular hour (4:6, 52) that Jesus makes his remark about his food being to complete the Father's work (4:34). Once completion has been stated in Christ's final words on the cross, the water flowing from Christ's side (19:34) then becomes the sign of that completion and of the pending fulfilment, in the resurrection, of his words to the Samaritan woman concerning the spring of water gushing up to eternal life (4:14).

We then hear that "the hour is coming, and is now here, when the dead will hear the voice of the Son of God, and those who hear will live" (5:25), followed by yet another time reference a few verses later, but now slightly different—"the hour is coming when all who are in their graves will hear his voice and will come out" (5:28–29). This seems not only to suggest that there are two types of "dead" being spoken about, figurative and literal, but also pre-empts the famous words later on from the raising of Lazarus, "Lazarus, come out!" followed by the command, "Unbind him, and let him go" (11:43–44). Once again, the parallel of *is coming* and *is now here* demonstrates the declarative authority of Jesus's time over our time.

Next there is the explicitly distinguishing phrase of Jesus to his brothers in Galilee near the start of chapter 7, "My time has not yet come, but your time is always here" and, two verses later, "my time has not yet fully come" (7:6, 8). This is now the third time we have an instance in John in which two references to time occur in quick succession of one another. The Greek of 7:8 also uses a tense which implies that once Jesus's time *does* fully come the effects will be enduring. A little later the fact that "his hour had not yet come" also prevents hands being laid on him while teaching in the temple (7:30, repeated in 8:20).

There is then a big turning point when Jesus enters Jerusalem, at the very start of the passion narrative, which the church commemorates at the beginning of Holy Week. Some Greeks express a desire to see Jesus, and just after the Pharisees have declared that "the world has gone after him." It is at *this* point that Jesus declares,

"The hour has come for the Son of Man to be glorified" (12:20–23), and immediately after this comes the fittingly seasonal and therefore time-relevant imagery concerning the grain of wheat that must fall into the earth and die if it is to bear "much fruit" (12:24). This idea, especially in relation to the Son of Man reference, will be explored further in the next chapter.

A few verses later, and as the point at which hands will be laid upon him approaches, along with the heralded hour, Jesus's "soul is troubled" but he explicitly decides against asking to be saved from the hour in question (12:27). The hour has also come with the judgement that the Father gives to the Son, including the driving out of "the ruler of this world," and alongside this we hear Christ's declaration of his power "to draw all people [or things]" to himself when he is "lifted up from the earth" (12:31–32). We should notice that here it is from the *earth* rather than the world that he is lifted up, accompanying the reference to the grain of wheat falling "into the earth" (12:24). This is followed soon after by a repeat mention that Christ came to save rather than to judge, but now with the additional observation regarding the power of the word spoken to act as judge in itself, especially "on the last day" when things are drawn to completion (12:47–48).

Jesus already knows before the Passover festival that his hour has come (13:1) and this hour comes to a fuller realization at the point of his betrayal, which is simply followed by the words "it was night" (13:30) and immediately after that by the assertion, "Now the Son of Man has been glorified, and God has been glorified in him" (13:31). There is something that the action of the *Logos made flesh*, specifically in the world and operating within time, is able to draw out, even through the darkness, that will transform the manner in which the creation, as new creation, comes to relate both to time and to the light. This makes it all the more fitting that the hour is subsequently opened up and likened to a pregnant woman's labor pains (16:21), transitioning into the joy of a new emergence through something achieved in the world but not being in this case of the world.

The hour is then said to be coming when Christ will no longer speak to the disciples in figures of speech, but tell them "plainly of the Father" (16:25). The rather presumptuous response of the disciples in this case has already been remarked upon, upon which Jesus in turn insists, "The hour is coming, indeed it has come, when you will be scattered" (16:32), which both repeats the now familiar Johannine idiom concerning time and simultaneously provides a deeper underlying context for the true *drawing in*, post-scattering, that the Father will effect through the Son when he is raised up from the earth, enabling the new growth from the buried grain.

Then we reach the great divine speech in which the Father is addressed directly by the Son, "Father, the hour has come; glorify your Son so that the Son may glorify you" (17:1), and the address itself lasts for the whole of chapter 17. The significance of the hour is, as it were, now raised to the level of divine and eternal discourse, and the relation to the world is consequently transformed. As Christ's hour is then completed in his finishing declaration on the cross (19:30) a new time is opened up, the seeds of which we can already hear pre-empted in the preceding note that "from that hour the disciple took her [Mary, the mother of Jesus] into his own home" (19:27, also recalling 16:32 at this point).

Here we may recognize another beautiful interconnection in John, relating to the first mention of Christ's hour back in chapter 2. Jesus has said to his mother, in relation to the running out of the wine, "Woman, what concern is that to you *and* to me?" (my italics, 2:4). The Greek text itself actually places things the other way around—"to me and to you"—and maybe the use of the word "and" here is just a reflection of how the phrase would naturally occur in the Greek. To an English ear, however, it strikes me that there is a subtle difference between saying "to me *and* to you" as opposed to "to me *or* to you." The latter might suggest that there is no real relevance of relationship involved, just a sense of "why should either of us care?" The former, however, could be read rather more as genuinely asking about the relevance of the fact in question to something that *both parties* concerned have in common, something that either does already relate them or will yet come to do so. In the relation in question Jesus takes the priority—"to me and to you"—but Mary has an implied share in it. In this case the relevance is projected *forwards* onto the pending completion of Christ's hour, a concern for Christ's time rather than for the purely here-and-now earthly time of his followers, noting Christ's remark in 7:6 once again. On this way of looking at things, Mary's response, saying to the servants, "Do whatever he tells you" (2:5), also makes very good sense if she somehow recognizes in Jesus's remark that she and others are to be caught up in the relevance of the hour in question.

As a final but fitting irony therefore, when the completion of the hour in question is imminent, Jesus points to a new relation, which would come to relate to the church more generally, symbolised by the taking of Mary into the home of the beloved disciple "from that hour." This is immediately followed by him declaring, "I am thirsty" (19:27–28). At this point the presence of *wine* returns in an unexpected and, in earthly terms, very bitter manner. A "jar full of sour wine" happens to be in the vicinity and they give him some of it to drink (19:29). There is a stark contrast here to chapter 2, in which Christ provides the "good wine" that has been kept until the end, until the completion of the hour, and for the true marriage banquet of the Lamb, so that it may be tasted by others. Now however, in the pivotal, darkly ironic, and fulfilling moment at the cross, Christ is given *sour* wine by the world. In fulfilment of the sign at Cana, however, Christ simultaneously shows himself as the true bridegroom who gives the good wine, even in his own blood, over to the sampling of the stewardship of the church, remembering that it is the chief steward who tastes the wine first (2:8–9). This tasting or sampling aspect to our stewardship sustains our *journey* of discipleship, and allows us to appreciate the bridegroom's accompanying presence, the beginning of a new family, and the preparation of a new dwelling-place.

THE JOURNEY CONTINUES

The idea of a journey is emphasized especially when Jesus says to those who had come to believe in him, "If you continue in my word, you are truly my disciples; and you will know the truth, and the truth will make you free," carrying an obvious emphasis on future continuation into what they do not yet know or appreciate fully (8:31–32). When he is then challenged by reference to his audience being descendants of Abraham, and therefore not slaves, he emphasizes that slavery is to sin and that a slave does not remain permanently in the house but only the Son (8:33–36). The journey therefore needs to move forward to the point where Christ later says to his disciples, "I do not call you servants [in the Greek the word used more usually translates as "slaves"] any longer, because the servant [slave] does not know what the master is doing; but I have called you friends, because I have made known to you everything that I have heard from my Father" (15:15).

There is a notable contrast, both in content and possibly in tone, between this and having earlier told those who questioned his questioning of their freedom that, while they may be "descendants of Abraham," there is "no place" in them for his word. While the Son declares according to what he sees in relation to the Father, those questioning him should reflect upon what they "have heard" in relation to their conception of their father figure (8:37–39, and it is noteworthy here that there is a textual variant in which some sources have "the Father" at this point while others have "your father"). There seems to be something about the accepting attitude of the disciples that makes the making known of that which Jesus has received from the Father a gift, and a declaration of friendship, rather than a weighty, ever-lingering question about the relation between their freedom and what is being heard and understood. That is *not*, however, to deny that there is much more that the disciples will need to come to understand, but there is now something far more guided and gifted about the process of doing so, even under difficult circumstances, and especially given the assurance of the Advocate.

The Horizon of Faith

The journey has two main dimensions: on the one hand it is a journey looking outwards and forwards to the greater that is yet to come—the subject of the next chapter—but on the other hand it is also a journey inviting people further *inwards* into the love and mystery of the Trinity, alongside a greater and deeper appreciation of themselves and their place. It is fitting in this regard that Christ removes his outer robe before he washes his disciples' feet and then also has to emphasize to Peter how important it is that this invitation is accepted, so that Peter *allows* his feet to be washed (13:4–8). This invitation becomes an exhortation when Christ subsequently says that if he, their "Lord and Teacher," has done this, then they should continue the practice among one another. The master is always greater than the servant and the sender of the messenger greater than the messenger (13:13–17). There is always further to go, more to learn, explore, and partake in. Furthermore, to receive a messenger is to receive the one who sent them (13:20). The journey is then further opened up with the giving of the commandment to love one another, just as Christ loves us, accompanied by the declaration that the disciples *will* now be able to follow Christ to where he is going (13:34–36), once again a development of the relational dynamics on Christ's initiative and say-so.

A grand closing summary of the overall contours of the journey is then echoed, after the resurrection, in the mention of Peter, having been naked in the boat, covering himself before jumping into and moving through the waters to meet Christ on the solid ground of the shore, followed by the boat with the other disciples and the symbolic catch of a hundred and fifty-three fish—the world now being seen through a rather different lens (21:7–11).[2] The idea of Peter being naked in the boat and only then putting

---

2. Moreover, the net is "not torn" so there is no subsequent need to mend it (21:11). Although not in John, it is perhaps noteworthy here that, in the other gospels, Jesus tells Simon Peter and Andrew that he will make them fishers of people, and when he subsequently calls James and John, the sons of Zebedee—also noted in John as being present in the boat when the third resurrection appearance occurs by the Sea of Tiberias—they are at that point in the process of mending their nets (Matt 4:18–22; Mark 1:16–20, with a somewhat different relating in Luke 5:2–11).

clothes on to jump into the lake might at first sound the wrong way around. Whatever the precise reasons, however, the *allegorical* note is very stark if we recall the nakedness recognized in Eden, the covering that the man and the woman require as a result, the waters of the flood and of baptism, the boat as symbolic of the accompanying support necessary for the church (or proto-church) to remain afloat on her journey towards the ultimate solidity of her destination, the disciples within her, the net and the fish echoing different aspects of the church's activity, and of course the Christ by and towards whom all is moved to find both solid ground and solid food. This speedily described activity of Peter therefore carries a great raft of symbolism and beautifully represents the bigger picture of the journey of faith in the church. At this point it is highly appropriate that Jesus does not say, "Come and see" but instead "Come and have breakfast" (21:12)—come and *sample*, come and *taste*. As a final note here, the ongoing journey continues to be emphasized right to the last, with Christ's final words to Peter being simply, "Follow me!" (21:19, 22).

I began this chapter with mention of the immersive experience of Holy Week. The immersion in our relation to the Anointed One, the Christ, develops continually and consistently in John, always looking to what is both before us and beyond us where the locus of primary relevance is concerned. One could say, overall, that in John we find rather more an unfolding of what is at first implicit than a series of events, although events are of course still witnessed to in John and the nature of that witness is explored in various ways.

It is especially worth considering, at this point, that John takes a relatively ambivalent attitude regarding the need for signs. On the one hand there is the clear framework of the seven signs, around which most of the pre-passion section of the gospel is constructed. On the other hand, Jesus is exasperated that, "Unless you [plural] see signs and wonders you will not believe" (4:48) and, in the context of the mention of the sign of the manna in the wilderness, he challenges people's understanding of the true significance of this event, which is already in front of them and they don't see it correctly (6:30–36). He later tells his accusers explicitly, "even though you do not believe me, believe the works" (10:38), and shortly after this we hear the acknowledgement of many that "John [the Baptist] performed no sign, but everything that John said about this man was true" (10:41). Later there is an observation that despite him performing "so many signs in their presence, they did not believe in him" (12:37), and in Jesus's words to Philip the recognition of mutual indwelling of Father and Son is given as the real crux of what is being driven towards in the gospel, while just believing "because of the works themselves" is presented rather as a second-best option (14:11). Finally, after the resurrection, Jesus then tells Thomas, "Blessed are those who have not seen and yet have come to believe" (20:29).

For John it seems very much a question of the trees being potential distractions from the context of the entire wood. They are necessary as scaffolding placeholders in the narrative at key stages in its development but, paradoxical though it may sound, the *whole* is ultimately the *focus*. This is somewhat counter-cultural in the modern world, a world often seeking a particular "tree" or point of focus with respect to which something can *clearly* be seen and said in worldly terms, while fearing the "whole" as being vaguer, less precise, or even in itself the distraction from proper focus on that which can more controllably be described. In John the disciples are to be caught up in the relationality involved rather than, so to speak, the "data" amassed at various points along the way. They are to follow, to grow, to discover, and to transform.

John certainly seems to me a helpful accompaniment for both the ethos of the journey overall and a means of keeping forward focused without unhelpful distraction. Even that which is difficult to journey through is, in John, part of the means and process by which joy can ultimately be made complete. As the next chapter will now consider in more depth, there is something distinctively, and perhaps even surprisingly efficacious about enduring and journeying *as flesh, as human nature, as mortal existence*—something that the divine nature can transform by way of a unique, divine-human victory and enhancement. This is "something" ultimately *greater* than what would, or even could, otherwise have been the case.

Chapter 5

Something Yet Greater
Openness to the Unfolding Beyondness

SEEKING MORE AND SUSTAINING FAITH

How often do you ask the question, either to yourself or to others, "Surely there is more to it than this?" Maybe you find yourself in a situation that is not what you expected it to be, or not what you had been led to believe it would be. Maybe others seem to be able to get excited about it, but you just can't. Maybe there is far too much repetition or insufficient evidence of success or affirmation. You might search for greater depth, greater assurance, greater interest, or greater motivation. Even if we *are* convinced of being truly part of something obviously greater than us, are there not still times when we think that the signs of this could or should be stronger than we necessarily perceive them to be, especially when things get tedious or the need for endurance is pushed towards our natural limit?

To my mind there is another thread that is notable in John, very much touching on this question of there being something *greater*, and in a manner that might perhaps reformulate the mentality with which we look at it, or indeed look for it. It won't solve all our practical earthly problems, but it is a thread that can perhaps

The Horizon of Faith

enhance the lived experience of faith and one that places a fitting final layer of consideration on the gospel in question. This layer is based upon the fairly frequent mention, explicitly and implicitly, of that which is both greater and yet to come, and also upon its grounding in the midst of shared, fleshly experience—that which is already here in some sense, recalling the idiom with which John treats time in relation to Christ. Sometimes we see the translation "greater things" but we should note that "things" is not explicit as a separate word in the Greek, which we might bear in mind as we consider this thread in John. I therefore refer to the "yet greater" in the title to this chapter.

Right from the outset in the Prologue we hear emphasis on life being in the Word, the *Logos*, who is also the light which is not overcome (1:4-5). What will unfold is therefore in this sense a positive guarantee, and the Prologue overall summarizes what ought to be anticipated in highly condensed form. The sense of this being greater than first imagined is arguably hinted at in the verse, "From his fullness we have all received, *grace upon grace*" (my italics, 1:16). This verse comes directly after the very strong implication of a new creation and new beginning, having its seed sown in the very mention of the *Logos* becoming flesh and tabernacling among us (1:14), and the insertion of John the Baptist's testimony that the Son "ranks ahead" of him because he was before him (1:15). An unfolding of that which is greater is to be anticipated in the new creation, and it hardly even needs mentioning, so obvious should it seem, that Jesus has "a testimony greater than John's" (5:36) from the outset.

The first explicit mention of "greater things" is Jesus telling Nathanael, whom he has already seen under the highly symbolic fig tree, that he "will see greater things than these" (1:50) and refers immediately afterwards to heaven being opened—a language strongly associated with some deeply meaningful vision or insight and therefore connected with the contemplative anticipation symbolised by being under the fig tree. Christ then adds mention of "the angels of God ascending and descending upon the Son of Man" (1:51). One thing I find intriguing about the layout of events here is that Nathanael has already just declared Jesus as the Son of God. This statement is made explicit three times in the opening chapter (1:18, 34, 49) and strongly implicated back in 1:14. To our ears this may sound like one of the highest and strongest titles we could possibly ascribe, emphasizing Christ's divinity. Curiously therefore, when Jesus then mentions the *greater* things that will be seen, he follows it with mention of the Son of Man rather than the Son of God. Admittedly this fits with the aforementioned theme of the variety of titles given to Christ early on in John, but in this case I genuinely wonder whether—in fact, it is perhaps better to say I strongly suspect that—the greater things that are referred to here are, by implication, *what they are* precisely because Christ is *both* Son of God *and* Son of Man together, the tabernacling *Logos* in human form, the Word made flesh.

THE SON OF MAN: A SHARING IN HUMAN FORM

A quick note is in order here on the title "son of man." Without a definite article attached to it, such a phrase is used many times in the Hebrew Scriptures and seems to have three main implications: firstly, as an expression of humble status as a creaturely mortal with respect to God; secondly, as an acknowledgement that one is a person, human offspring, rather than some other animal species; thirdly, in ascribing to a human creature some kind of eschatological significance—a significance lying beyond this present world or sphere of existence that can also become involved in effecting a completion and transformation of it. This is sometimes associated with a Messianic figure.[1]

It is in the New Testament that this phrase acquires a definite article, becoming *the* Son of Man, and in John especially this says as much about origin ("where from?") as it does about destiny or eschatological fulfilment ("where to?"), but it still retains an inseparable association with the matter and place of creaturely status

---

1. See for example Bible Gateway, "The Son of Man," paras. 2–3.

and created dwelling. Moreover, it imparts to such status a greater relevance, something that moves through and motions beyond all earthly generations for God's greater purpose. It is notable that, in all but one instance in Acts 7:56, the occurrences of the phrase "the Son of Man," with definite article,[2] are from Jesus's own words in the gospels. It has been speculated that he uses the phrase simply to denote "I" or "me," though a later view has been that the phrase speaks of "the humility of Christ's incarnate manhood as contrasted with the majesty of His Divinity [sic] denoted by 'Son of God', and as emphasizing His universalist role as 'son of Adam' in contrast with the nationalist conceptions associated with the title 'Son of David.'"[3] It is certainly in this sense of distinctiveness in relation to Christ's divinity and to his humanity that the phrase "the Son of Man" will be taken in what follows here.

The next explicit mention of the Son of Man after Jesus's encounter with Nathanael comes in chapter 3, when we hear Jesus telling Nicodemus, "If I have told you [plural in the Greek, therefore indicating the Jewish leaders in general] about earthly things and you do not believe, how can you believe if I tell you about heavenly things?" (3:12). This is then paralleled with mention of the Son of Man and the Son of God, notably in the reverse order from that found in chapter 1. Jesus first emphasizes the Son of Man as the only one to ascend into heaven because he is also "the one who descended from heaven" (3:13), and thereby the means by which a specific revelation or communication can be revealed to mortals. He then compares the lifting up of the Son of Man to Moses lifting up "the serpent in the wilderness" (3:14-15). This refers to the story in Numbers 21:4-9 in which the people speak against God and against Moses about the absence of water and proper food in the wilderness, so the LORD sends poisonous serpents among them. When the people ask Moses to "pray to the

---

2. There is a mention of "one like a son of man" at the opening of the vision in Revelation 1:13, and while the NRSV actually imports a definite article at this point in the translation it is *absent* in the Greek.

3. Cross and Livingstone, *The Oxford Dictionary of the Christian Church*, 1529.

LORD to take away the serpents" the LORD commands Moses to make a fiery serpent (of bronze) and to lift it up on a pole, so that anyone bitten by a serpent could look upon the bronze serpent and live. This reference is especially fitting in John, as the gospel emphasizing Christ as the true living water and the bread that came down from heaven—the proper and eternal nourishment—as well as the one to be lifted up on the cross and ultimately to ascend to the Father.

Jesus then proceeds to tell Nicodemus of the depth of love involved in God giving "his only Son" and of the pivotal importance of believing "in the name of the only Son of God" (3:16–18, cf. 1:12). In chapter 1 the mention of the Son of Man comes after mention of the Son of God and occurs in conjunction with the image of heaven being opened and the angels of God *ascending and descending* upon the Son of Man. This links up very smoothly with the subsequent mention of the Son of Man himself *descending and ascending* into heaven in chapter 3, before returning to further mention of the Son of God. The image of the ascending and descending may also bring to mind the famous story of Jacob's ladder or stairway from Genesis 28. Interestingly, in chapter 4 of John, Jesus encounters the Samaritan woman at "Jacob's well" (4:5–6), which, although not mentioned explicitly in the Old Testament, does certainly indicate depth and a *drawing up* from the depths (cf. 4:11), not least in a sense related in some manner to history and to that which has already in some respect been laid down or received. At the very least this is a fitting complement to the imagery of coming down from the heights and then returning to them.

Between these explicit mentions of the Son of God and Son of Man in chapters 1 and 3 we encounter some hefty implication of that which is yet greater to come in chapter 2. First, we have the famous story of the turning of the water into wine at the wedding at Cana, notably "on the third day," which might already point towards a sense of transformation in the resurrection—also the first day of a new week—and to that marriage feast of which Christ himself is the bridegroom. Let us consider the layout of this narrative:

(a) *Mention of Jesus, his mother and his disciples, along with reference to place* (Cana) *and time* (third day) (2:1–2).

(b) Mary tells Jesus that *there is no wine left* and Jesus questions Mary as to what concern that is of theirs, followed by reference to the fact that his *hour has yet to come* (2:3–4).

(c) *Mary instructs the servants* to do whatever Jesus tells them (2:5).

(d) Mention of the *six stone water-jars* associated with purification rites (2:6).

(c) *Jesus instructs the servants*, "Fill the jars with water ... draw some out, and take it to the chief steward" (2:7–8).

(b) Mention of the chief steward tasting the wine, calling the bridegroom, and exclaiming surprise that the good wine has been *saved until* this relatively late point. The *wine is restored* in a manner beyond expectation and the phrase "until now" effectively parallels the "hour" in verse 4 (2:9–10)

(a) *Mention of Jesus, his mother and his disciples, along with reference to place* (Cana and then on to Capernaum) *and time* (remaining in Capernaum "for a few days") (2:11–12).

We can see that there is a clear sandwich structure to this narrative and that it pivots around the mention of the six stone water-jars in verse 6. On first viewing we might think this is quite a bland central point for the narrative, until we consider the number symbolism involved. The number six stands for imperfection and incompletion, something awaiting completion through a particular initiative of which, in this case, only God is capable. Christ notably stands alongside these jars. He is by implication the *seventh jar* and one that is not made of stone but of living flesh, bringing forth the water that will subsequently be mentioned as welling up and giving eternal life (4:14 again) and *completing* the Father's work in a new creation, according to a new rite of purification. Moving towards the *yet greater* to come involves a rich foretelling of pending completion at this point. We might also remind ourselves here of the consequent fittingness of the Samaritan woman later leaving her water-jar with Jesus on the mountainside (4:28).

The wedding narrative is then immediately followed by the account of Jesus driving the traders out of the temple, fittingly at a time when the Passover was approaching, and the prophecy regarding the coming of a new temple *in three days*, with an explicit clarification to all readers that Christ's body is in this case being referred to (2:13–22). We may note in this case another instance of number symbolism when Jesus's remark concerning the destruction and rebuilding of the temple in three days is met with the objection that it "has been under construction for forty-six years" (2:20). Forty is idiomatic of a long time and six, once again, of incompletion. Just like in the preceding wedding narrative, we encounter again the theme of a need for completion ultimately lying beyond the capacity of human labor alone, even over a long time.

On the subject of labor, it is also worth noting at this point, returning to the encounter between Jesus and the Samaritan woman at the well, that when the woman asks him where he would get the living water of which he speaks she immediately follows with the question, "Are you *greater* than our ancestor Jacob?" (my italics, 4:12). She then asks him to give her the living water so that she "may never be thirsty or have to keep coming here to draw water" (4:15). Jesus has literally just assured her that this water—the spring of living water that he will cause to well up in those who hear his word—will permanently quench thirst (4:13–14), but there is clearly a difference between this water and that literal water which she will have to labor to continue drawing.

This distinction is emphasized in the fact that, in response to her request, Jesus turns the topic back to the question of *knowledge*. He has already told her, "If you *knew* the gift of God, and who it is that is saying to you, 'Give me a drink', you would have asked him, and he would have given you living water" (my italics, 4:10). He now demonstrates his powers by indicating *his knowledge* that she currently has a man who is not her husband and that she has previously "had five husbands," which convinces her that he is a prophet (4:16-19).[4] He then adds, "You worship what you do not know; we worship what we know" (4:22). This yearning for true knowledge, and its eventual acquisition, is effectively what connects the depths and the heights that have been noted previously.

Jesus will, of course, also proceed to show to the Jewish authorities of the time, and others, precisely what they do *not yet know*, what they have not received or understood in the proper way, so there is a tone of irony here too, but the point of the encounter in question is to emphasize an opening to all true worshippers to "worship the Father in spirit and truth" (4:23 again). Human laboring will be necessary in some way or another right to the end, but something that it cannot ultimately reach or complete is nonetheless being offered to us, just as the disciples are subsequently told that they are sent to reap the fruits of the labor of others, and that they "have entered into" that labor (4:38). When the Samaritan woman then tries to show what she *does* know—"I know that Messiah is coming . . . When he comes, he will proclaim all things to us"—it is then the perfect entry point for the first of those explicit phrases of Jesus beginning "I am" (4:25-26).

In chapter 5 we then hear Jesus's declaration that the Father will show the Son "greater works than these, so that you will be astonished"—in other words, greater works than the signs with which the Jewish authorities are taking issue (5:20). Interestingly, this is followed closely afterwards by another dual mention of Son of God and Son of Man: the first occurring in the context of the dead who "hear the voice of the Son of God" and live (5:25); the second noted specifically in relation to the authority of the Son "to execute judgement, *because* he is the Son of Man" (my italics, 5:27). This is a judgement in one sense *of* creation, but in an even more significant sense *in* creation, and through a word and voice that is inseparable from the *Logos* through whom creation came about

---

4. I wonder here whether the fact that she is now somehow with her sixth man, who is technically not her husband, might also contain a hint of number symbolism, needing a seventh form of relationship in order to find true completion, which Jesus is in effect offering. That is pure speculation of course, but, given some of the other subtleties of John, I feel drawn to consider the possibility.

in the first place. The preposition "in" is especially important in relation to a *sharing in humanity* upon the Word becoming flesh, emphasized in reference to the Son of Man and to the outworking and execution of judgement, while the voice giving true life still issues from the divine personhood of the Son of God.

Although not explicitly heralded under the heading of greater things, the closing section of chapter 5 sows a further significant seed in this regard. Jesus says to the Jewish authorities, "You search the scriptures because you think that in them you have eternal life; and it is they that testify on my behalf. Yet you refuse to come to me to have life" (5:39–40). In one sense this points to the fact that the people whom Christ addresses were not, to his mind, viewing the scriptures in the proper manner. They did not, or could not, see and interpret with the necessary depth and insight. This, of course, is not merely a problem of the time in question, but part of a continuing challenge—a journey of searching, digesting, and interpreting. The challenge remains the case in our own day, in an age that sometimes seems to idolize simplicity and straightforwardness no matter how much of a distortion or oversimplification it might be. But there is a yet deeper challenge afoot here, as we should by now expect from John. Effectively, Christ questions the apparent *disjunction* between the manner in which the scriptures are collectively regarded as reflecting the Word of God and the more particular capacity for insightful recognition of him as the *incarnate* Word.

This identity is not to be trivialized, since among other things it requires rather different forms of attention to be paid in each case: on the one hand, attention to a flowing, embodied, and contextually-embracing form of living interaction that necessarily involves an overall journey; on the other hand, a textually focused, theological-landmark-seeking, and position-defining attention that might possibly come to accept only *one* way of receiving revelation in written form. No matter how well-meaning and vehement in its enthusiasm, this latter form of attention-paying always runs the risk of becoming potentially static, a seeking of stability-as-stasis.

The Horizon of Faith

Christ masterfully highlights something of the nature of this risk when he proceeds to say, "I have come in my *Father's* name, and you do not accept me; if another comes in his *own* name, you will accept him" (my italics, 5:43). This remark points to a lack of willingness, or perhaps even witting-ness, properly to recognize or acknowledge that there must be an *inner life* of God that is intrinsically *dynamic*, flowing, and creatively communicative. This would, of course, later be made manifest in the threefold doctrine of the Persons of the Trinity, co-habiting within and co-motioning towards each other, inhering in a self-*containing* unity whilst equally *maintaining* proper distinctiveness among the Persons of Father, Son, and Holy Spirit. This is the basis of the greater life that can draw us into itself as active participants. It is very fitting, given the challenge posed here by Jesus, that it is also in John that we find the bulk of the biblical evidence for moving towards an explicit doctrine of the Trinity, interestingly along with other literature of the New Testament ascribed to someone called John—thinking especially of the First Letter of John and the Book of Revelation.

Christ also adds, however, that he will not act as accuser, since the attitude adopted towards the scriptures in this case effectively stops short of him, as it were, through a failure to appreciate what is being pointed towards. He therefore declares that "your accuser is Moses, on whom you have set your hope. If you believed Moses, you would believe me, for he wrote about me" (5:45–46). A deeper realization of truth needs to unfold, namely truth as unfolding and *non*-concealment, *a-lētheia* in the Greek (14:6, among other places, in which the prefix *a-* indicates a negation of what follows, in this case a negation of being obscured or concealed). This idea is further and rather ironically expressed in Pilate's question, "What is truth?" (18:38). In the context of Jesus's trial, the question seems at first a rather unexpected philosophical interlude, for which Pilate tellingly waits for no explicit response. Instead, he goes out and initiates the pivotal moment in the real unfolding of the truth standing right before him in the flesh. As an interesting aside on this, Bill Bryson, in an entertaining section on wordplay in his book *Mother Tongue*,[5] notes the Roman world's historic fascination for wordplays such as anagrams, with a classic example apparently having been *Quid veritas est?* ("What is truth?"), which is an anagram of *Est vir qui adest*, meaning, "It is this man here." Given that Latin was presumably Pilate's mother tongue, make of that what you will!

Truth, as opening and non-concealment, has an eternal quality. Consider then that the next mention of the Son of Man occurs as part of an exhortation by Jesus not to work for perishable food, "but for the food that endures for eternal life, which the Son of Man will give you. For it is on him that God the Father has set his seal" (6:27). Not only does there seem to be a link here between the seal and the fullness of the image of God in the incarnate Word, but also, in terms of Christ's sharing in human context, there is even a resonant connection between material, time-bound creaturehood and eternity. The connection is made in the Son of Man who is also the Son of God, and something about the *sharing* in human context specifically makes even the eternal food in question *what it is* for us. I use this phrase deliberately, since the mention of "manna" in Exodus 16:15, of which Christ stands in fulfilment in John, is sometimes translated via the question "What is it?" including in the NRSV. Something concerning the nature of the food in question needs contemplating.

The connection reaches its climax at the point of explicit identification between the bread that will be given "for the life of the world" and Christ's flesh (6:51), subsequently described a couple of verses later as "the flesh of the Son of Man" (6:53). This proves to be rather a dramatic turning point as it furthers the grumbling discontent that has already started to brew. Matters have now become, for some people, very uncomfortably focused in a form of explicit identification to which they were totally unaccustomed and hence the complaint even among the disciples, "This teaching is difficult; who can accept it?" (6:60). Christ responds to this by further appeal to the Son of Man, this time to his ascending, remembering again at this point the encounter with Nicodemus in

---

5. Bryson, *Mother Tongue*, 222–27.

chapter 3. Specifically, Jesus asks, "Then what if you were to see the Son of Man ascending to where he was before?" (6:62) and further points to the fact that the flesh can only give life if it is inseparable from "the spirit" (6:63), which in the Son of Man it is. Indeed, we might be right to capitalize the word Spirit at this point, although there is no explicit identification made in John with the Holy Spirit at this point, and the NRSV retains a lower case here.

To modern ears this might sound like an unwelcome expression of dualism between matter and spirit, even perhaps some form of animism, but in the context in question it simply emphasizes that, however we read the term "spirit" in this case, the context for the unity of the two is situated in Christ, Son of God and Son of Man together. The life-giver and the life-given are in union, and this mysterious union—or, to use the official doctrinal term, the *hypostatic union*—between divinity and humanity is the fundamental source from which all those "greater things" in John unfold. Further on in the gospel we hear yet another emphasis on the significance of the lifting up of the Son of Man, specifically where acquiring *realization* is concerned (8:28), again with the implication of something greater to unfold.

Just as the Samaritan woman had asked Jesus whether he was greater than her people's ancestor, Jacob, so the questioners of Jesus in chapter 8 ask, "Are you greater than our father Abraham, who died?" (8:53) and they repeat the question as to *who* exactly he is. This provokes the unbridled response by which Jesus, through the direct and unqualified use of the words "I am" (8:58), applies to himself words reserved for God alone, famous from the narrative with Moses and the burning bush (Exod 3:14), and certainly not to be spoken in this manner according to the custom of the time. Stones are immediately picked up in anger (8:59) and Jesus *hides himself* and, again rather symbolically, leaves the temple. The very language of hiding suggests something yet to be unfolded or revealed, something that G. K. Chesterton once described as that which Christ "covered constantly by abrupt silence or impetuous isolation…some one thing that was too great for God to show us" even in dwelling or tabernacling among us on earth, and he adds the potent suggestion that this "some one thing" might possibly be Christ's "mirth."[6] That is not intended as an authoritative statement of course, but I reference it here because it does carry a certain poetic intrigue, and not without precedent given Dante's choice of *Divine Comedy* for his own poetic title.

Then, in chapter 9, Jesus finds the man born blind whose eyes he has opened, whom the authorities have also just cast out for presuming to teach them, *outside the temple*. We may note the development and contrast here with respect to Jesus earlier having found the man he healed at the pool in chapter 5 *in the temple*. The man whose eyes he has opened represents a new context of encounter, beginning to move into the new understanding of the temple pointed towards back in chapter 2. Jesus fittingly asks the man at this point, "Do you believe in the Son of Man?" (9:35), to which he quite understandably replies, "And who is he, sir? Tell me, so that I may believe in him" (9:36). Very appropriately once again, given what has been said about both seeing—insight, understanding—and speaking, or testimony, being key themes in that newly opened freshness of vision for which this anonymous man stands, Jesus replies, "You have seen him, and the one speaking with you is he" (9:37, cf. 4:26). The planted seed is shared, ready to spread and germinate into the yet greater, and it is shared specifically with the one who bears the sign of the new vision. There is transformative potential in this renewed way of seeing, a way of seeing that is still truly and fully *human*, and one that will *come* to see (cf. 1:39), appreciate, and testify to the fullness of humanity as God intended it, taken up into the life of God in the Son of Man.

In a similar vein, the implication of the yet greater is also clearly present in the phrase "I came that they [the sheep] may have life, and have it *abundantly*" (my italics, 10:10) and then, more explicitly, we hear that the sheep will never be snatched away because, "What my Father has given me is greater than all else" (10:29). The whole of the yet greater is contained within the givenness and the giftedness of the Father-Son relation, once again in the translating

---

6. Chesterton, *Orthodoxy*, 155. He actually finishes the book in question on this thought.

of the Author's immutable Idea according to a *particular form of expression*, through a centering on a Principal Actor, a particular manifestation of Activity, depending on whether we emphasize the analogy of Balthasar or that of Sayers. This occurs in a manner drawing the audience and the other actors in—the "sheep" in this case. There is a similar tone expressed at the end of the passage in which Christ describes himself as the vine and his disciples as the branches, at which point he declares that he has said this to them "so that my joy may be in you, and that your joy may be complete" (15:11). Both this and the above mention of having life abundantly echo the earlier mention of the one who "gives the Spirit without measure" (3:34).

In chapter 12, there is then the mention of the hour of the Son of Man's glorification, in this case emphasizing the physical agony and suffering of the approaching passion, and the accompanying image of the dead grain of wheat falling into the earth in order to bear much fruit, the greater things that are yet to germinate. Once again, we have here an overlap of more than one Johannine theme—the hour and the greater things—combined in one pivotal turning point explicitly referencing the Son of Man (12:23–24). The pending glorification of the Son of Man is then accompanied by the *double* exclamation in response to Jesus saying, "Father, glorify your name," which meets the heavenly reply, "I have glorified it, and I will glorify it *again*" (my italics, 12:28). The glory will be manifest not only in the divinity of Christ, as Son of God before the creation was brought into existence, but also in the humanity of Christ, as Son of Man, in what is about to occur. This is further highlighted by the two distinctive but united aspects of the glorification that I mentioned previously regarding the opening verses of chapter 17: the glory relating to the authoritative work given to the Son within creation and that relating to the Son's eternal status with the Father (17:1–2, 5). A few verses later this distinction is made even more explicit and *participative*, when the Son says to the Father, "All mine are yours, and yours are mine; and I have been glorified *in them*" (my italics, 17:10). Once again, the use of the past tense gives an eternal quality to this address.

The concept of the Son of Man continues to cause confusion, however, and just as the man born blind has asked previously who the Son of Man is, so at the pivotal point in chapter 12 the entire crowd repeat the same question (12:34). Jesus's response is that they should walk while the light is available, while they have the benefit of seeing God and humanity, Son of God and Son of Man, in union in Christ before their eyes. The time will come when people will no longer see so directly, and will therefore have to seek deeper and more implicit ways of appreciating Christ's presence among them and navigating their discipleship. Fittingly therefore, immediately after Jesus has told them to walk while the light is relatively obvious, we hear yet another *hiding* reference—"he departed and hid from them" (12:35–36).

TOWARDS A GREATER BEHOLDING

The need to seek deeper and greater means of seeing, understanding, and appreciating is immediately developed in what follows. We are presented with a declaration of fulfilment concerning some words of the prophet Isaiah (12:38–41), specifically Isaiah 53:1 and Isaiah 6:10. The first of these comes from a section of Isaiah pre-empting the pivotal figure of the Suffering Servant, and it is part of a text often traditionally set as one of the readings on Good Friday. The second follows directly on from the famous temple vision of Isaiah 6:1–8 in which the prophet receives his calling. The first asks, "And to whom has the arm of the LORD been revealed?"—a question clearly dependent on the manner in which something is received and believed, and what might happen as a result of this receiving. The second considers what happens in circumstances when people are actually *prevented* from seeing and comprehending properly *until* some critical occurrence has occurred—something that can provide a strong enough basis for a deeply meaningful and lasting transition, a true change of heart and mind. When and how such a transformation or critical transition might be expected to take place is then a natural question, and the follow-on verse in Isaiah 6:11a therefore has the prophet ask, "How long, O Lord?" and the response is:

> "Until cities lay waste without inhabitant, and houses without people, and the land is utterly desolate; until the Lord sends everyone far away, and vast is the emptiness in the midst of the land. Even if a tenth part remains in it, it will be burned again, like a terebinth or an oak whose stump remains standing when it is felled." The holy seed is its stump.
>
> (Isa 6:11b–13)

These words speak of a total and utter renewal that requires a thorough stripping out prior to a fresh revelation, highlighting the true seed and foundation of what is yet to spring forth. We might indeed cross reference Isaiah 43:19 at this point, with its mention of the "new thing" that "springs forth" and the accompanying question as to whether people *actually* perceive it. This is followed immediately by the famous reference to "a way" being made "in the wilderness" and "rivers in the desert."

Overall, the people are ultimately forced to see and consider in a manner that they previously did not, or perhaps even could not. Possibly eyes and hearts had in some cases been so set on one particular way of beholding and thinking that they had become blind and impervious to anything else, and something needed to happen that gave no option but to be shaken out of this mindset in order to journey forward. Some critical transition was needed in order to evoke a particular turning towards a new vision, and the scene encountered in the climax of Christ's passion as commemorated on Good Friday is then the fulfilment of this need for thorough, radical renewal. This is indeed the true sense of the word "radical"—from the Latin word *radix*, meaning "root"—in that it really gets to the root of the problem and what is needed to resolve it, namely the real and unencumbered flourishing of the holy seed.

In fact, in the verse directly *preceding* the first of the Isaiah verses mentioned in this section of John, namely Isaiah 52:15, we hear of one who "shall startle many nations; kings shall shut their mouths because of him; for that which had not been told them they shall see, and that which they had not heard they shall contemplate." If we compare this with another classic Good Friday text, Psalm 22, we could also say that the new seeing and new hearing is itself what makes for a *new people*, as the final verse of the psalm refers to a proclamation in the future to "a people yet unborn." In respect of what Christians see as the new covenant in Christ, which at the time was *yet* to be brought forth, this is both literal and figurative in its reference to birth, which may further remind us of Jesus's words to Nicodemus earlier in John (3:3, 5).

For all that has just been said about Good Friday, it is important therefore that the proclamation, "*Now* the Son of Man has been glorified, and God has been glorified in him" (my italics, 13:31b) occurs just after Jesus's betrayer leaves the company of the others in order to seal Christ's earthly fate and prepare the great and paradoxical climax of Good Friday (13:31a). Rather like those images that talk about the glory of the Lord, and about the Son of Man coming through a context of "clouds and thick darkness" (Ps 97:2; Isa 60:2; Dan 7:13–14; Matt 24:29–30; 26:64; Mark 13:24–26; 14:62; Rev 1:7), so here the moment of glorification occurs just after it is stated that "it was night" (13:30). Access to habitual ways of seeing and navigating is symbolically blocked at this point of imminent transformation.

In chapter 14 we then hear Jesus explicitly preparing the way for the sharing of, and participation in, that which is yet greater, when he tells the disciples that "the one who believes in me will also do the works that I do and, in fact, will do greater works than these, because I am going to the Father" (14:12), which is followed later in the same chapter by the declaration that "the Father is greater than I" (14:28). I have already remarked on this in relation to the distinction made by Sayers between the "essence" of the Author's Idea and its specific form of "expression." All that is *drawn in* by the expressing of the Idea participates in the drama and forms an additional dimension to the dynamics of glorification (17:10 again). In fact, the process of being drawn in is in itself what affords us the possibility of true and proper participation. There is a similar tone in Jesus's later remark to his disciples that "it is to your advantage that I go away, for if I do not go away, the Advocate will not come to you" (16:7). Here again, the parallel with the analogy of the stage drama, where the world is part of the stage as Balthasar describes it, is very revealing. If participants in the drama are too reliant on the explicit physical presence and lead of the Principal Actor then they will not have a proper appreciation of the important role of the Director, who allows for the *depth* of the drawing in that is involved to become more apparent.

In the theological context, things remain centered on the Principal Actor in the sense that the dynamics of expressing and of drawing in other participants—as actors and as audience—to himself are still *choreographed* with his role. Nonetheless, it is his "going away," his retreating to a domain in which he can only *indirectly* be discerned, that forces the participant onlookers into a new means of beholding his presence. This involves more attention being paid in relation to the Idea and to the overall sense of Authorship, to the meaning that it communicates and to the form of response that it ought therefore to evoke in and among the various participants who are drawn in. While the Authorship remains something that is pointed towards through the Principal Actor, the indirect nature of the Actor's accompaniment now requires a correspondingly greater alertness to the role of the Director, the Advocate for the Idea and for the proper manner of its expression and its evoked response among participants. Here again we find in John the idea that there is further for the participants to go, that there is something yet greater to be beheld in not being reliant on being able to see the Son directly before our eyes, a widening of *horizon* towards the greater things to be completed, and something that will unfold further the depth of the Father-Son relation in the Spirit. Among other things, the place of creaturely initiative and activity is thereby significantly *empowered*.

In chapter 15 reference is directed back to the giving of the new commandment to love one another, which originally occurs just after the declaration of "now" with respect to the Son of Man's glorification in chapter 13. Jesus repeats this command and then declares, "No one has greater love than this, to lay down one's life for one's friends" (15:12–13). Here we encounter the intensely powerful suggestion that, in respect of the *power* of such self-sacrificial love, even the yet greater finds its limit.[7] Such a boundary has already been pre-empted in chapter 13, in the reminder that "servants are not greater than their master" (13:16). In chapter 15, even *after* Jesus has told his disciples that he no longer calls them servants (15:15), this reminder is repeated a few verses later (15:20). That *nothing* ultimately surpasses what can be contained by such self-sacrifice puts both the nature and the holding together of the yet greater in stark context—something that is in one sense demonstrable *in* the world but is not *of* the world because it is ultimately empowered by something beyond the world. Again, we may compare this to the very closing verse of the gospel in relation to the world, considering that *part* of the stage that we can somehow contain among ourselves, but always as held in *participant* relation to that which we cannot.

In chapter 16 Jesus then declares, "I still have many things to say to you, but you cannot bear them now" (16:12). Some things can only be borne, beheld, and appreciated after the ultimate demonstration of self-sacrifice, and this capacity to bear is immediately related to the "Spirit of truth" who "will guide you into all the truth [again, *alētheia* in the Greek]" (16:13). The word "guide" fits with the analogy of Holy Spirit and Advocate as Director, and the double meaning in English of the word "bear" is also rather convenient here—being directed such as to *find our proper bearing* makes possible the bearing of that which would previously not have been bearable. In Matthew 11:28–30 we are famously told that Christ makes the bearing of our yoke light, and the yoke was both a wooden crosspiece—with very obvious symbolic relevance in a Christian context—and a means of *directing* the ploughing of a field, gathering in a harvest. An established means of guidance

---

7. Donald Nicholl even goes so far as to say, on the subject of self-sacrifice, that, "No being, neither man nor God, can go any further." Nicholl, *Holiness*, 13.

towards the bearing of the yet greater is made manifest, not least through material symbols, in our midst.

BEYOND THE RESURRECTION: THE WIDER HORIZON OF FAITH

It is of course to be expected that the emphasis on that which is yet greater points through to the reality of the new life in the resurrection, and once we find ourselves on the other side of the resurrection, as it were, the yet greater aspect to things is presented in an intriguingly subtle manner. Before going any further, however, we should note three small details. First, just as the declaration of the moment of glorification of the Son of Man occurs just as night has fallen (13:30), so the first moment of encounter with the reality of the resurrection dawn occurs "while it was still dark" (20:1). Second, we should remember the mention of "the cloth that had been on Jesus' head" that is "rolled up in a place by itself" (20:7), a wording which reminds me somewhat of the scroll with the seven seals that needs to be opened and unrolled in Revelation 5:1–5, remembering also the previous mention in John of the "seal" set on the Son of Man (6:27).[8] Not only the sense that there is more to be unfolded, but furthermore the question of who carries the power to do so seems relevant here. Third, even Jesus's addressing of Mary Magdalene is new, in the sense that it is the *only* time in the whole gospel that he explicitly addresses a woman by name (20:16). These three briefly mentioned and hence easily overlooked aspects already set the scene before we come to the meat of what is involved from 20:19 onwards.

Even amidst fear and closed doors, Christ appears to the disciples and gives them *his* peace (20:19, 26), but again *not* in a worldly sense (14:27). Personally, whenever I hear this narrative, including the account of Thomas, having at first been absent, demanding to see the risen Christ and to feel the marks of the nails for himself, necessitating a repeat appearance (20:24–29), I always

---

8. The same Greek word for seal is used in both places.

Something Yet Greater

think of another narrative, namely that of Noah's Ark. In that story—another story of thoroughgoing renewal—an ark is constructed in order to *protect* those inside from the mighty waters of a flood (Gen 6:11–22). The instructions given for building the ark might, in terms of the style of their presentation at least, remind us of those given for the construction of the sanctuary beginning in Exodus 25, and the description of Solomon's construction of the house of the LORD in 1 Kings 6. The link with the creation as a whole is further implicit in the three-story, triple-decker nature of both the ark (Gen 6:16) and the house of the LORD (1 Kgs 6:6), perhaps paralleling the three tiers of creation in the biblical world: seas, earth, and heavens.[9]

Noah is then told to enter the ark along with pairs of animals representing the created order more generally (Gen 7:1–3), and while "all the fountains of the great deep burst forth, and the windows of the heavens were opened" (Gen 7:11) all who are to enter the ark with Noah go in and *the* LORD *himself shuts Noah in* (Gen 7:16). As the waters swell the ark rises high above the earth, while all else is swept away, and then "God remembered Noah" and makes "a *wind blow* over the earth" such that the waters subside (my italics, Gen 8:1). Once the waters subside and the ark comes to rest on the mountains Noah then waits forty days—the "long time" in Hebrew idiom—and finally opens "the window of the ark" (Gen 8:6) and sends out a raven which roams about without finding a resting place (Gen 8:7). Next, he sends out a dove, a bird that is also well known as a *symbol of the Holy Spirit* resting upon Christ (Matt 3:16; Mark 1:10; Luke 3:22; John 1:32). At first, however, the dove finds no solid ground on which to rest, so returns to Noah (Gen 8:8–9).

Noah therefore *waits for seven days* and sends the dove out again, and this time the dove returns, "in the evening," carrying

---

9. This is all the more interesting as a possibility when one further considers that, in the 1 Kings account, the lowest story is five cubits wide, the second six cubits wide and the third seven cubits wide. Parallelled with the days of creation in Genesis, the fifth day is that on which the sea creatures are made, then land-dwelling creatures on the sixth day, then the declaration of completion concerning the seventh day.

the proverbial olive leaf, which has in turn become a recognized symbol of *peace offering* (Gen 8:10–11). Finally, he *waits for a further seven days* before sending the dove out a third time, whereupon it no longer returns (Gen 8:12) as it has presumably found *solid ground on which to rest.*

Given the huge allegorical significance of the story of Noah, and especially seeing in Noah something of a scriptural prefiguring of Christ, the events of the resurrected Christ's repeated appearance to the gathered disciples in John rather intrigues me if held in parallel with the story in Genesis. First of all, it is in this case the *disciples* who have, superficially speaking, *shut themselves inside* the protective space in question, locking the doors out of fear (20:19). It is then *Christ*, the incarnate LORD, who *opens* some alternative means of entry—some mysterious "window" of which the disciples are unaware—for the bringing both of *peace* and the *gift of the Holy Spirit* into that place, further noting that it is also in the *evening* that this occurs (20:19) and that the Spirit is breathed onto them by Jesus in conjunction with the classic imagery of *wind* and *breath* that we find elsewhere in the scriptures, and very notably in Genesis. The italics here should make the suggested and, to my mind at least, rather intriguing comparison clear—though I am not of course commenting on whether this parallel was in any respect intentional.

Thomas's absence then causes a demand for a repetition of this appearance under the same circumstances, including a repetition of the offering of peace, *seven days later* (20:26). Thomas expresses a need for physical evidence, rather like the olive leaf being a tangible sign of the subsiding of the waters. He needs to see and feel the physical evidence of Christ's presence and scars if he is to believe. Yet the question remains as to whether this is sufficient to find and appreciate more fully the true *solid ground* that is ultimately sought as a resting place—that indicated in the final and unreturning release of the dove into the new context of the post-flood world. Jesus's response is to allow Thomas the evidence he needs, but further to follow this up by declaring, "Blessed are those who have not seen and yet have come to believe" (20:29). The fuller realization of a final solid ground is something lying somewhat beyond this first evidencing, something *yet* to be brought to the full completion of its expression by being *fully inhabited*. It is very fitting in this case that in the Noah's Ark story *another seven days* is waited before sending the dove out for the third and final time, seven being the number associated with completion. We should also remember that, in the Old Testament context, there is a clear distinction between the leading of the people towards the Promised Land, under Moses, and the entering and occupying of it, under Joshua.

Tangible evidence is important, but just as the dove in the Genesis story ends up not visibly returning, which also signals the time to leave the ark and to enter into the new context of life on the far side of the flood, so too there is something altogether greater implied in Christ's words to Thomas. The resurrection life is to be explored more deeply, by *way of which* the disciples are to learn in a deeper and higher sense—one that is not directly or trivially visible—to discern and feel the ongoing, developing contours of Christ's presence among them. They are to explore the resurrection body in the church more fully and thereby more profoundly to "feel out" their own indwelling part in the new temple that *is* the resurrection body and the food of eternal life (recalling 2:19–22 and 6:51–58). Personally, I hear in this great challenge and invitation of Christ a renewed and transformed sense of the exhortation in Psalm 48:12–14: "Walk about Zion, go all around it, count its towers, consider well its ramparts; go through its citadels, that you may tell the next generation that this is God, our God for ever and ever. He will be our guide for ever."

The New Jerusalem and New Zion is to be explored in a higher and deeper sense, which is also echoed in the open-ended manner in which John finishes, in supposing that, were everything that Jesus did—and *still does*—as the *Logos* made flesh, died, risen, ascended, and glorified, as Son of God and Son of Man together, to be written down, then the entire world would not contain the books that would be written concerning the Activity of that Word which is ultimately beyond all words.

That would, in one sense, be a very good tone on which to finish, and indeed the end of chapter 20, just after Jesus's words to Thomas, constitutes a "first ending" in John (20:30–31), with the overall ending of chapter 21 subsequently reinforcing it and adding to the scope of its claim. Chapter 21 might seem like a subsequent insert, but there is still a bit more to say concerning this chapter in relation to the yet greater to come.

First of all, we can remind ourselves of the fact that the previously repeated exhortation and invitation, "Come and see" is replaced by, "Come and have breakfast" (21:12a). Something that has already been seen, felt, and recognized anew is now *tasted*, which may remind us of those famous words, "O taste and see that the LORD is good; happy are those who take refuge in him" (Ps 34:8). It is equally notable here that they no longer ask, "Where did you come from?" or "Where are you staying?" or even "Who are you?" Instead we are told that they all just "knew" (21:12b). There is also a nice reference back to the feeding narrative in John 6, which has already prefigured the idea that there is yet greater to come, when the resurrected Jesus now distributes bread and fish to the disciples (21:13).

We then hear an implicit mention of a progression towards greater things, when Jesus asks Peter three times whether he loves him and, for the first time of asking, whether he loves him *more* than the others (21:15–17). Not only does this parallel Peter's previous denials of Jesus but it also allows for a developing commission to be made: first, "Feed my lambs"; second, "Tend my sheep"; third, "Feed my sheep." There an obvious progression here from infancy to maturity, lambs to sheep, in the faith and journey of discipleship, but there is also a notable switch of accompanying verb. The first and the last, "feed," are the same Greek word, *boske*. The second, "tend," is the Greek word *poimaine*, which can also mean to herd and at root means to act as a shepherd for. There are notably two stages of feeding, sandwiching the tending, which we may perhaps hold in parallel with the distinction between milk and solid food made in Hebrews 5:11–14 and also by Paul in 1 Corinthians 3:1–4. The experience of transitioning into a mature faith is then a matter of tending and shepherding, and that which is greater and yet to come is strongly connected with such growth and maturity.

I can't help also perceiving at least a faint, but interesting similarity between the oscillation of verbs here—*boske, poimaine, boske*—and that found earlier in the same chapter in relation to the drawing in *towards* Christ of the catch of fish commissioned *by* Christ. This moves from the *inability to haul the net into the boat* (21:6), through the *ability to drag the net behind the boat* in the water, not too far from the solid ground of the shore (21:8), to Peter's sudden *ability to haul the net ashore* (21:11). In this case the oscillating pattern of verbs in the Greek is similar—*helkusai, surontes, heilkusen*—with the first and the third instances having the same root.

There are two components to the journey here, both being a matter of *developing in capacity*. One is maturity and the other is the strength to bring the catch to where it needs to be, once again something commissioned by Christ towards Christ. These components are obviously related to one another, and with Peter explicitly involved in both instances, hence the interesting nature of the overlap in terms of how they are presented over three stages. To return to the very closing verse again, keeping this journey towards both maturity and destination in mind, brings us finally to reflect on the insufficiency of the world to contain the overall result—something which, in terms of analogy, can only be beheld in reference to the greatest love of all, in which respect Peter is also to "follow" in Christ's example (21:18–23). To appreciate *now* the true nature of the yet greater that is to unfold, is precisely to reflect on the relation of the form of such to the form of glorification of the Son of Man in his full humanity, as first hinted by Jesus to Nathanel at the end of chapter 1.

There is something utterly pivotal about the *human* aspect of the divine-human union and dynamic. Despite its total inferiority to divinity overall, this humanity nonetheless brings, through its God-gifted and image-bearing capacity for searching, discerning, appreciating, and following, through all the various moods and circumstances of life, a *distinctive bearing* upon the manner in which the yet greater unfolds into a *fuller inhabiting of a new context of containment and contentedness* in the Word beyond all words. The Creative Activity of the *Logos*, the house of the Father (14:2), in whom such containment occurs, cannot adequately or exhaustively be described within our current domain of existence. It is in this Way that we are directed towards an ultimate realization of a completeness of joy together. That is the sense of greater depth to our containment and contentment towards which the developing narrative of John directs us, as well as pointing to a form of resource that may sustain us in those times when we feel the pressing need to seek more than there might seem to be in our lives at present. The horizon of faith remains ever open.

Epilogue

Tension and Ambiguity in John

Given the many interconnections between the various threads in John, it should be expected that a few tensions or possible ambiguities will surface—tensions that we need to find a healthy way of living with, in a way that keeps our view of the gospel alive and engaged. To my mind, some of the possible tensions are as follows:

1. A tension between references to "all," on the one hand, and only to those who believe, receive and do as they ought, or only as the Father allows to be drawn to the Son, on the other.

2. A potential contrast between Jesus's words, "Do not sin any more, so that nothing worse happens to you" (5:14)—clearly a very tall order and also seeming to imply that suffering, including the man in question's previous suffering, is in some way connected with sin—and the later assurance to the disciples that the man who was born blind was *not* in the state that he was either because of personal or parental transgression (9:3). Similarly, we hear Jesus say to the woman caught in adultery, "Go your way, and from now on do not sin again" (8:11) and yet also challenge her accusers to cast the first stone only if they themselves are without sin, which, of course, they are not. This statement is notably sandwiched by repeated reference to Jesus writing something in the dust on the ground (8:6–8). Dust represents that from which, in

material terms, we came (Gen 2:7), and also that to which mortals return, as reflected in the words traditionally said upon the imposition of ashes on Ash Wednesday. In John it will also subsequently be used to make the mud by which Jesus opens the eyes of the man born blind (9:6). We should further note that the question of sin posed specifically in relation to the man born blind is also used as a deliberate contrast to when the authorities later presume him to have been "born entirely in sins" and object to the idea of his sudden capacity to see and his audacity to presume to teach them (9:34). This objection is subsequently turned on its head when they ask Jesus a few verses later, "Surely we are not blind, are we?" and meet with the reply, "If you were blind, you would not have sin. But now that you say, 'We see', your sin remains" (9:40–41). This highlights the stark contrast in John between genuinely seeing and *presuming* to see—a contrast echoed in Jesus's words, "I came into this world for judgement so that those who do not see may see, and those who do see may become blind" (9:39).

3. There is arguably also some tension with regard to the nature and degree of creaturely initiative, especially with respect to how efficacious it is. On the one hand there are all the things that Christ alone knows, does, and pronounces without reference to, or help from, anyone aside from the Father. On the other hand, there are the variously allotted capacities for the different followers to see, hear, engage, and question in their own way and to call others alongside them, including the tone of openness to that wider horizon on which the gospel, as a whole, finishes.

4. We might also reflect on the nature of the containment or the "boundary" of our dwelling place as on the one hand holding together and, on the other hand, a form of separation and division between within and without. The Greek is interesting at this point. The word *chōris* indicates being apart, without, separate, or distinct—and similarly for the

corresponding verb, *chōrizō*. The word *chōros* is similar, but more specifically indicates a defined space or allotted area such as a piece of ground, a particular region, etc. There is a bit of an overlap between the two, and the former can also be used in the sense of a distinctiveness of allotment where place is concerned—for example, when we hear about Jesus's headcloth being rolled up in a place *by itself* in the empty tomb (20:7). It is clear, however, that there are subtle differences depending on context, not least because to be distinct is not the same as being separate, considering the doctrine of the Trinity for a start! Furthermore, the Greek word *perichōreō* is one that has had great influence on trinitarian thinking, with the word "perichoresis" describing the inseparably co-related and co-dwelling motioning of the Persons of the Trinity. If we alter this Greek word just very slightly, we get the word *perichoreuō* meaning to dance around, and you may well have heard reference to the trinitarian "dance" for that reason. The *chor-* part to this latter word in particular is what gives rise to the English word choreography. Choreographed dancing is about making suitable space for the other in conjunction with an overall flow or directing motion, hence the suitability for talking about the Trinity. In a more negative vein, but involving a similar principle in the Greek text, Jesus tells the Jews who claim to be no one's slave, protesting their freedom as Abraham's descendants when he suggests that the *truth* needs to set them free, that "there is no place" in them for his word (8:37). In other words, they seem to have sought their own distinction to the point of separation.

5. On a related note, we also hear in John (10:16) that there is one "flock," *poimnē* in the Greek, but that not all members come from the same "fold," *aulē* in the Greek, in this case indicating an enclosed form of abode. This flock is to be drawn into one house according to Christ preparing a place for those who would hear and follow (14:2). The opening out of the enclosures and the transformation of place is a

key theme in John, once again indicating the horizon of a new form of containment.

Tension can always be present in the way that we hear things, of course, especially if something seems to pull us simultaneously in more than one direction. Some tensions genuinely need quick resolution, but others are more inevitable and enduring, such that it actually becomes part of good spiritual practice to learn more effectively to live with them and to incorporate them responsibly. In bearable quantities tension can in fact be an effective and positive source of motivating energy. What we do not need, however, is a violent, "let's just sort this out right here and now for ourselves" approach to this latter type of tension, since then, rather like Peter wielding his sword and cutting off the ear of Malchus, "the high priest's slave" (18:10), a distorted and lopsided hearing will result. Furthermore, since listening and obedience are strongly interrelated concepts, an unstable and ill-balanced response is also likely to ensue.[1] I mention this as a parting thought because it is important that our reading and reception of the gospel, and other sources of theological sustenance too of course, is kept alive, balanced, and fresh, given the depth and breadth of the horizon that lies open to our explorative engagement.

---

1. As an aside on this, there is a possibility that Malchus—whose name is from the Hebrew word for king, and possibly means "my king"—may have had his ear pierced as a sign of his slavery, following the injunction from Deuteronomy 15:12–17. This then poses the question of freedom and to whom he really belongs. To whom should the phrase "my king" apply? It is unlikely that this naming is coincidence in John, but from Jesus's response to Peter it is clear that the issue is not effectively dealt with by cutting off the ear, which will not bring about a proper response—one that is suitable to the type of freedom that is to be found in Christ. I must express gratitude here to Fr Victor Feltes for his very revealing article on the "Parishable Items" website, which first drew my attention to this interesting dimension regarding the possible Deuteronomy link. Feltes, "The Meaning of Malchus," paras. 2–4.

Bibliography

Aland, Barbara, et al. *Novum Testamentum Graece.* 27th ed. Stuttgart: Deutsche Bibelgesellschaft, 2001.
Balthasar, Hans Urs. *Theo-Drama: Theological Dramatic Theory,* Vol. 1, *Prolegomena.* San Francisco: Ignatius, 1988.
Barrow, John D., and Frank J. Tipler. *The Anthropic Cosmological Principle.* Oxford: Oxford University Press, 1986.
Bible Gateway. "The Son of Man." https://www.biblegateway.com/resources/encyclopedia-of-the-bible/Son-Man.
Bryson, Bill. *Mother Tongue: The Story of the English Language.* London: Penguin, 1990.
Chesterton, G. K. *Orthodoxy.* Peabody, MA: Hendrickson, 2006.
Christian, David. *Origin Story: A Big History of Everything.* London: Penguin, 2019.
Christian, David, et al. *Big History: Between Nothing and Everything.* New York: McGraw-Hill, 2014.
Cross, F. L., and E. A. Livingstone, eds. *The Oxford Dictionary of the Christian Church.* 3rd ed. Oxford: Oxford University Press, 2005.
Davidson, Benjamin. *The Analytical Hebrew and Chaldee Lexicon.* Peabody, MA: Hendrickson, 2007.
Feltes, Victor. "The Meaning of Malchus." Parishable Items, Mar. 21, 2024. https://parishableitems.com/2024/03/21/the-meaning-of-malchus/.
Grondin, Charles. "What Is Nathanael and the Fig Tree About?" Catholic Answers. https://www.catholic.com/qa/what-is-nathaniel-and-the-fig-tree-about.
Levenson, Jon D. *Sinai and Zion: An Entry into the Jewish Bible.* New York: HarperOne, 1987.
Liddell, Henry George, and Robert Scott. *Greek-English Lexicon: With a Revised Supplement.* Oxford: Clarendon, 1996.
Nicholl, Donald. *Holiness.* London: Darton, Longman and Todd, 2004.
Sayers, Dorothy L. *The Mind of the Maker.* New York: HarperSanFrancisco, 1987.

BIBLIOGRAPHY

Williams, Rowan. *Open to Judgement: Sermons and Addresses*. London: Darton, Longman and Todd, 2003.
———. *The Truce of God*. London: Fount Paperbacks, 1983.

www.ingramcontent.com/pod-product-compliance
Lightning Source LLC
Chambersburg PA
CBHW070454090426
42735CB00012B/2547